D0907309

Keepers of the Children

Keepers of the Children

Native American Wisdom and Parenting.

Laura M. Ramirez

Walk in Peace
Productions

Keepers of the Children
Native American Wisdom and Parenting
by Laura M. Ramirez

Walk in Peace Productions
POB 12396
Reno NV 89510-2396

Unattributed quotations at beginning of chapters are by Laura M. Ramirez.

Publisher's Cataloging-in-Publication
(Provided by Quality Books, Inc.)

Ramirez, Laura M.
    Keepers of the Children : Native American wisdom and parenting / Laura M. Ramirez.
    p. cm.
    Includes bibliographical references.
    LCCN 2004100588
    ISBN 0-9748661-0-5

    1. Parenting. 2. Parent and child. 3. Child development. 4. Moral development. 5. Indian philosophy--North America. I. Title.

HQ755.8.R36 2004   649'.1
                          QBI04-200040

Cover photo by Laura Ramirez. Cover design by Robert Howard.

Table of Contents

**Chapter 7: Teaching Your Child to Thrive
in a World of Surface Charms** 166

Blessings and Acknowledgments

Life is a process of *becoming*. Many people have helped me become the person I am today—the kind of person who could write this book. After I had finished it, I realized that it wasn't so much the book itself, but the person and parent I *became* while writing it that has given me a lasting sense of joy.

First, I want to thank my wise husband, Larry, who taught me many of the Native American concepts in this book. He has been the leaping-off point for the development of my own ideas and provided solid ground on which to land. My husband is my confidante, my hero and the great love of my life. From him, I have learned the importance of working toward my dreams. Due to my mule-like stubbornness, I know that life with me has not been easy. On some level, though, I believe that my husband suspected what he was in for from the start. In fact, when he first met me—he told my mom that I was "like a diamond in the rough"—I just needed "a little polish." Little did he know how much polishing I would require. Although at times it must have been tiresome, he was heartened by the occasional glimmer. My husband's love and generosity have taught me what it feels like to be known and cherished and how to know and cherish others in return. For me, there has been no greater gift of love.

I give thanks to my two sons, Dakotah and Colt, for their irrepressible spirits and pure, sweet hearts which have burst open my own. I thank them for their patience with my writing; for curling up next to me each morning, giving me morning-mommy hugs and sweetly, but firmly prying the notebook computer from my hands. Their love has shined into my heart and made it whole. I am grateful to my children every day for teaching me how to be a mother.

While my husband encouraged me to fly, my parents forced me to dig deep. Although I grew up in what most would call a dysfunctional family, I am thankful to my parents for providing the childhood experiences that have given a sense of urgency to the concepts in this book. I have come to realize that my mother and father did the best they could and that without the circumstances of my childhood, I

9

would not have developed the perspective to write this book. Thank you, mom, for the day you told me that I could write and compared my work to a well-known writer. Although I was almost forty at the time and had been struggling for years, your words gave me the boost I needed. On the flip side, thank you, dad, for discouraging me. I'll never forget when I was a teenager and you became angry when you discovered that I had been taking the bus to the park to write. You thought writing would get me nowhere. Although this moment caused me to diverge from my chosen path, ultimately, it led to an insider's understanding of why parents must encourage the gifts inside their children's hearts.

I thank my brother, Mike, for the many hours he spent with his ear glued to the phone, listening patiently as I read him my first attempts at writing stories. I'm sure that listening was as painful as my struggle to trust my writing.

I am indebted to Erik and Joan Erikson for their theory of human development. Although they died many years ago, their work lives on. I reference their work extensively in Chapter 6 and hope that in some small way I have responded to Joan's invitation in her book, *Wisdom and the Senses*, to continue the work that she and her husband started.

To Arlene Williams: thank you for your encouragement and guidance. Your gently framed suggestions have given shape to this book. Although at first, I resisted your idea to use Native American myths to illustrate some of the abstract concepts in this book, doing so has created substance where it was lacking. To Pete Adams: many thanks for your technical expertise. I will always remember the day I received the first copy of the galleys that you and Arlene had generously printed out and sent me in the mail. As I tore open the manila envelope and flipped through the pages, I exclaimed out loud, "Wow! It looks like a *real* book!"

To Robin Nelson, my soul sister: your friendship has been a source of joy and inspiration. Special thanks to my friend, Kim Hotchkiss, who helped me with my online business which gave me more time to write.

I am grateful to the anonymous male subscriber who sent me an email a few years back that said, "If you ever write a book, I'll be the first in line to buy it." I wish I still had your email address, so I could thank you personally and remind you that it's time to pull out your wallet!

I feel a great debt of gratitude to Native Americans and indigenous people around the world. I hope that you will not be offended by the ways in which I have borrowed and re-framed some of your cultural ideas, instead, I hope that you will celebrate the sharing of this wisdom. I want to thank you—*the people*—for beliefs that honor life and reveal the many ways in which the Creator shows Himself through nature.

I give humble thanks to the Force that fills my heart with words which flow like water from my brain. It is this Force that whispers the insights I share with you.

Last but not least, I thank you, the reader. This book is my prayer to you—to the families and children of the world. May the words fall softly on your ears and may you make them yours in a way that feels right to you. May you share your insights with your children and inspire them by the caring, respectful way in which you live.

Walk in Beauty,
Laura Ramirez

Preface

As a white woman married to a Native American man, my family is a mix of cultures. The parenting ideas presented in this book are a reflection of this cultural blend. In these pages, I have woven together an understanding of child development with little known Native American wisdom. The result is a unique blend of ideas that shows parents how to raise children to know their nature, hone their strengths and create lives of meaning, purpose and contribution. By helping children create fulfilling lives, parents deepen their sense of satisfaction with their own.

The Native American way is one of seeing, being and taking action in the world. It is a world of relationships and subtle understandings. Although certain chapters in this book explain native concepts in detail, other chapters have little more than a passing reference. While this may seem odd, it was intentional. I wrote the book in this way to underscore the basic gulf in thinking that has long divided the native culture from the white.

The best way to illustrate this gulf is by telling you a story. Before I do, allow me to explain the best I can. Culturally, white people are raised to see life through its denotation or literal meaning. White people learn what a thing is, what it does and what it means. By contrast, Native Americans are raised to see life's denotation *and* connotation—what something is, what it does and what it means *in relation to the whole.* Learning to see the connotation is about *making connections.* Making connections gives you a greater perspective in *all* areas of life, particularly with regard to raising children.

Now that I've explained the meaning (or denotation) of the gulf between white and native thinking, allow me to illustrate the *connotation* through real-life story. Five years after my husband and I were married, he told me that he was going outside to pray. Respecting his need for privacy, I left him alone for awhile, then went outside to ask him if he was hungry. I found him down on all fours beside our backyard waterfall, moving small rocks around to change the direction of the water's flow. As I approached him, I said, "What are you doing?"

Without taking his focus off the rocks, he replied, "I'm praying."

When most white people think of prayer, they see its denotation—an image of someone kneeling bedside or sitting in a pew with head bowed and palms pressed together. But to the Native American, prayer is a *way of being in the world.* It is an artful and compassionate way of living that is not limited to a particular body position, place or time. By arranging the rocks to change the direction of the water's flow, my husband was communing with God. The understanding that life *is* a prayer *is* the connotation. In this way, everything you do can be a nod to the sacred, especially the way in which you raise your children.

Although some people may protest that a white woman has written a book containing native ideas, my husband tells me that in many ways, I am one of the "most native people he has ever known." In the native world, such people are called "sycamores"—white on the outside, but red at heart. Since I understand that some people may have a problem with me dispensing ideas from a culture other than my own, I admit that my understanding is limited by the fact of my whiteness. At the same time, however, I invite my critics to see beyond the denotation to the connotation and find their *connection* to the ideas in this book.

What I offer in these pages is not an either-or perspective, but a blend of two cultures that celebrates the best of both. By combining a deep understanding of child development with Native American wisdom, we will raise a generation of children who know themselves and understand the nature of existence. Such children will grow up expressing their nature by contributing what is in their hearts.

While this book contains many resourceful parenting strategies and ideas, ultimately, it is a spiritual work. As you raise your child, your child inspires you to grow. It is who you raise your child to be *and* who you *become* in the process that will fill your heart the most. When this happens, you will grasp the connotation of parenting: *we are all keepers of the children.*

Walk in Peace,
Laura Ramirez

Introduction

To convey some of the essential concepts of parenting that will be covered in this book, I have written a story called *Spirit-Boy and the Gift of Turquoise*. It illustrates some common errors that parents make and how to correct them before it is too late. Since I will refer back to this story throughout the book, please make sure to read it.

A good story draws you in and immerses you in an imagined world. Since story evokes powerful images and feelings, it is the closest you can come to a lived experience without having to go through it. The following story offers the reward of insight without the risk, pain or struggle of real life. As you read it, ask yourself the question: *What kind of story am I creating for my child?*

Spirit-Boy and the Gift of Turquoise

Many years ago, there was a young, Native American man named Chato and his beautiful wife, Kevote. They loved each other deeply and longed to have a child.

When Kevote discovered she was pregnant, she led her husband down the path that wound along the river. Under the shade of a giant oak, she placed his hands on each side of her belly. His eyes lit up. She held his gaze and smiled. The river sloshed against a boulder and sprayed the air. A few feet from the river, the village bustled with activity, as men returned from a day in the fields and women ground corn or cooked tortillas in their kivas. Beyond the circle of hogans, red cliffs jutted above the desert floor and shimmered in the heat.

At sunrise the next day, Kevote and her husband exchanged gifts to celebrate. Chato reached inside his pouch and pulled out a green turquoise pendant that hung from a leather thong. He fastened it around her neck and traced the copper veins in the stone. "Our daughter will be just like you," he mused, "spirited as the mustang."

Kevote's eyes twinkled. She opened her palm to reveal a blue turquoise ring with a spider-web design in the stone. She took her husband's hand in hers, wriggled the ring past his knuckle, shook her head and smiled. "No—our son will be just like his father—swift and sure-footed, like the deer."

When Kevote showed the necklace to her mother and repeated Chato's words, Old Eyes smiled. "Your child may resemble you and Chato," she said, "but a baby is like a piece of turquoise. You must polish it to know its nature." She traced the copper veins in Kevote's pendant with her fingertip. "Your child will be as unique as the matrix in this stone."

When Kevote repeated what Old Eyes had said, her husband's face darkened. "Old Eyes is jealous. She is alone in the world without a husband and doesn't know our happiness." Kevote nodded. She snuggled into the crook of her husband's arm, fell asleep and had a dream.

In the dream, her grown son came to her—a handsome young man with shining eyes and long, black hair. His skin was coppery like his father's, but he had his mother's smile. Around his neck, he wore a stunning blue-green piece of turquoise—a mix of the two colors worn by both his parents. But what Kevote failed to see—or didn't want to see—was the jagged, lightning-bolt-shaped matrix that tore through the center of the stone.

Kevote awakened with the blue-green color vivid on her mind and shared her dream with Chato. "I had a vision of our son. He wore a piece of turquoise that was a blend of yours and mine. He will be like both of us. You are right—Old Eyes is envious."

When the baby was born, it was a boy who had the same eyes and coppery skin as the young man in Kevote's dream. Since he so closely matched her vision, she named him Spirit-Boy.

Chato and Kevote laced their newborn son into his cradleboard to prepare him for introduction to the tribe. One by one, the people came to visit.

When Old Eyes held her grandson for the first time, she peered into his eyes and smiled. "Welcome to the world, Spirit-Boy." She nodded at her daughter. "You have named him well." Her dark eyes glinted. She handed Kevote a deerskin medicine pouch drawn tightly by a leather thong.

"In the pouch is the boy's medicine. It is a gift for him, but also for his parents. Polish it with eyes that see into his heart. Keep it until he knows himself and finds his place among the tribe."

After the old woman left their hogan, Kevote loosened the pouch and dumped its contents into her palm. She was startled to see the vivid, aqua-colored turquoise of her dream. She showed it to her husband. "By giving Spirit-Boy this blue-green piece of turquoise, Old Eyes has admitted she was wrong."

The beaming parents rested by the fire and cradled their new-born son between them. "See his eyes," Kevote gushed, "they are as black as yours." Chato traced the curve of the baby's face and teased, "Look—he has his mother's stubborn little chin."

As Spirit-Boy grew, Kevote and Chato continued to find the many ways in which their son reminded them of each other. "See how fast he runs—as though the wind were at his back. Look how he stamps his feet when he is angry—just like his mother."

When Spirit-Boy was five, tragedy befell the family. Chato was fishing on a boulder by the river when storm clouds gathered overhead. Lightning struck a tree nearby and split it at the trunk. As it groaned and leaned toward him, Chato realized he was directly in its path. His only hope was to jump into the river. He took a breath and leapt. He surfaced for a moment, but the River Spirit sucked him under, dragged him to the bottom and crushed his head against the rocks. When Kevote saw the men pulling her husband's body from the river, she sank to her knees and howled into the pelting rain.

Before her husband's burial, Kevote removed his ring. One day, when Spirit-Boy became a man, she would give him Chato's ring. She slipped it on the thong alongside the green turquoise pendant. The pieces of turquoise clicked together, as they settled over her heart—a reminder of the love that the River Spirit had taken. From that day on, Kevote forbade Spirit-Boy from going near the river.

When he was eight years old, Spirit-boy crept up behind his mother. She sat cross-legged in the dirt, humming softly and grinding corn in a stone mocahete. As he lifted a bare foot to take another step, she sensed his presence and without turning, called out, "Y-e-s?"

Spirit-Boy stamped around to face her, raising little clouds of dust. He planted his feet, crossed his arms and announced, "One day soon, I will be a man."

Kevote bit her lip, but couldn't hide the glimmer in her eyes. She looked down, as she crushed the corn against the bottom of the mocahete with the weight of the grinding stone. "Yes, my son, you are getting bigger every…"

"And a man must provide for his family, right?" interrupted Spirit-Boy.

Kevote straightened. "Yes…"

He jumped up and down. "Then you'll let Dancing Hawk teach me how to fish?"

"No!" exclaimed Kevote. She gripped the stone.

"But mother," argued Spirit-Boy, "the River Spirit brings us food and water. To be a man, I must learn its ways!"

"No!" screeched Kevote. She pointed her finger. "Don't you say another word."

Spirit-Boy clenched his fists and stomped away. Concerned what he might do, Kevote followed at a distance. When she saw him leap into the river, she ran and plunged in after him. The frigid water stunned her and for a moment, she feared they both would drown. She paddled toward her son, but he kicked away. She overtook him. Gripping him around the chest, she pulled him toward the riverbank, as he tried to wriggle from her grasp.

On shore, she took him by the shoulders. "I've rescued you from the River Spirit and your foolishness!" she spouted, but her voice broke and her eyes spilled with tears. She smoothed back the hair that was plastered to Spirit-Boy's forehead. "I won't let the River Spirit take you too." Her eyes were wild; her voice was strangled. Spirit-Boy turned away. She took a breath, grasped his chin and turned him back to face her. "You are *so* like your father. His animal spirit was the deer. Deer drink from the river, but they do not *swim* in it."

Spirit-Boy stood up and crossed his arms. "I *like* to swim!" he shouted. "I like the feel of moving through the water. I am like the pike minnow, not the deer. One day, I will be strong enough to swim upstream—away from *you* and my dead father!"

Kevote winced, but when she spoke, her voice was soft. "You are young and do not know yourself. You were little when your father died. The more you grow, the more I see him in you."

Spirit-Boy clenched his fists. "I *hate* you!" he screamed and stormed off to his grandmother's hogan, where he spent the night.

As Spirit-Boy grew, so did his anger. He picked fights with other

17

boys for fun and treated adults with disrespect. The elders joked that his name should be changed to Attitude-Boy, but his destructiveness was no laughing matter. The only person who seemed to understand him was Old Eyes. He spent much of his free time with her.

One day, Kevote barged into her mother's hogan and demanded to know the whereabouts of her son.

"He's not here," said the old woman, her eyes fastened to the bead work on her loom. She did not want her daughter to know that she had let the boy go fishing.

"But he is *always* with you," protested Kevote.

"Perhaps because I know his heart," said Old Eyes gently.

"I know his heart!" countered Kevote. "It is *I* who love and feed him."

"You feed his body, but starve his spirit," said Old Eyes softly. "Go get his medicine pouch. I will show you."

Kevote stamped back home, took the medicine pouch from the keepsake box and brought it to her mother's hogan.

"Open it," urged Old Eyes.

Kevote opened the pouch and removed the turquoise stone. The blue-green color was as stunning as she remembered. She pressed the ring and pendant to her chest. "It hasn't changed a bit," she said, jutting out her chin.

"That's why your son is angry," replied Old Eyes, but she could see that her daughter didn't understand.

"Spirit-Boy may look like Chato and have his mannerisms, but his heart is *his*. I know you miss your husband, but by looking for him in Spirit-Boy, you fail to see your son. Get to know his heart. He's twelve—soon, it will be too late."

A lump was growing in Kevote's throat. She swallowed hard. "How?"

"Encourage what he loves. That's how you polish anything— with love and wonder." She stroked her daughter's cheek and smiled. "Remember… the rough-cut stone is to the gleaming piece of turquoise, as the boy is to the man."

For the first time, Kevote understood the meaning of turquoise. What she had encouraged in Spirit-Boy were the qualities he shared with Chato. She had lost her husband, but refused to lose her son. She placed the turquoise in the medicine pouch and made a promise to herself.

When her son came home that night, he smelled like fish, but she said nothing. Instead, she asked him about his interests. The more she listened, the more he told her. Over time, she came to know his heart. One day, she reached out and gripped his muscled shoulders. "Your upper body is big and strong. Surely, it can hold its own against the River Spirit."

Spirit-Boy beamed at her. He remembered the last time she had taken him by the shoulders. That day, her eyes had been wild with fright. Today, they shone, warm and constant as the desert sun.

Spirit-Boy's fifteenth summer was the happiest of his life. He swam in the river like a crazy fish. He fished with his friends, giving most of what he caught to the elders and the families of the boys he used to taunt. He challenged his friends to swimming contests which Kevote and Old Eyes often watched.

Spirit-Boy spent many hours studying the river's current. On some days, it was a rapid; other days, a stream. Although swimming had made his muscles big and strong, he knew that there were days on which the River Spirit was stronger. On those days, he nodded at its power and found something else to do.

Three months later, Old-Eyes and Kevote were gathering willows by the river's edge when the old woman slipped on a rock and fell into the rushing water. Kevote screamed, as she watched her mother tossed like a withered leaf downstream. Hearing the commotion up the river, Spirit-Boy plunged into the water. He fought hard to reach his grandmother and tried to keep her head above the water, as they struggled back to shore. They collapsed on the riverbank. Spirit-Boy cradled his sputtering grandmother. Kevote raced to them and flung herself at their side.

After she had tended to her mother, Kevote walked back to the river's edge and perched on a boulder. She hugged her knees to her chest, watching the movement of the water. Ten years ago, she had planned to give Spirit-Boy his father's ring on the day he proved himself a man. That day had come, but now she knew he needed something more.

As the sun's final rays swept across the horizon, Kevote strode to her hogan. Old Eyes was bundled on a pile of blankets. The fire sparked, as Spirit-Boy threw in a log. Kevote beckoned her son to his grandmother's bedside. She took the pouch from her keepsake box and removed her husband's ring from the leather thong. "Today you saved your grandmother's life. You have great courage, like your father…" She paused. Her eyes twinkled as she held his gaze. "But your heart is *pure* Spirit-Boy." She slipped the ring onto his finger.

Kevote removed the turquoise from the medicine pouch and was stunned to see a polished stone. She gasped, as she peered closer. In its luster, the matrix was clearly visible—a black, lightning-bolt-shaped vein that seemed to split the stone in two.

As she fastened it around Spirit-Boy's neck, she said, "You are like the lightning bolt that strikes the earth, bringing goodness to the soil. Your spirit is strong. Polish it and use it in service of the people."

Kevote grasped Old Eyes' hand and squeezed it gently. "You were right, mother—the turquoise was a gift to me as well."

Spirit-Boy and the Gift of Turquoise underscores many essential concepts of parenting that will be covered in this book. Some of these ideas will be unlike anything you have encountered. Now that the story has spoken to your unconscious, let the insights in these chapters feed your heart and mind. If some concepts seem unclear, keep reading—they will all come together in the end.

In this book, you will find a blend of two seemingly disparate ideas—Native American philosophy and developmental psychology. The merging of these philosophies creates a way of parenting that is grounded in the real world, yet spiritually based. These ideas will show you how to celebrate and encourage your child's uniqueness while fostering your growth as a parent and human being.

Chapter 1

Raising Your Child with Vision

Where vision lives, children flourish.

A Real-Life Story

When I think about the difference that loving parents make in their children's lives, I remember my encounter with the championship boxer, Oscar de la Hoya. At a promotional dinner in Las Vegas in November 2002, Oscar was posing for photographs with his fans. During a lull, I approached him for an autograph. As I handed him a poster of himself to sign, I said, "Oscar, write something you believe in."

He looked at me. "What do you mean… something I believe in?"

"A statement about something you feel is important in life."

"Something I believe *deep* down in my heart?" he asked, grinning boyishly and tapping his fist against his chest.

I nodded.

He signed the poster, then handed it back to me. Above his autograph, he'd written the words: "I love my MOM."

His eyes twinkled and I smiled in recognition. Oscar de la Hoya, who holds seven world titles in five different weight classes, had confirmed that his big heart was nurtured first outside the ring, in the loving light of a mother, who had encouraged her son to shine.

If you ever have the opportunity to watch Oscar box, you'll notice that at the end of the match, he looks up, opens his arms in a wide embrace and blows kisses to heaven. If you know his story, it's easy to see why. Oscar's mother died many years ago, but you are *alive* and whether you're a mother or a father, you have a chance to make as big a difference in your child's life as Oscar's mother made in his.

This is the subject matter of this book. By reading and making the ideas your own, you will learn how to create a lifelong relationship with your child that is based on love and mutual respect. Using a mix of Native American philosophy and developmental psychology, you will discover how to raise a child who *knows* himself, knows his purpose, fulfills his destiny and cherishes *you* for these gifts.

It is my deepest hope that one day your adult child will acknowledge you in the manner of Oscar de la Hoya.

The Story You Are Creating for Your Child

Oscar de la Hoya is a championship boxer and a living example of a man who attributes much of who he is today to his mother's love. Would you feel honored one day, if your adult child said the same of you?

Every parent would.

The first step in making this a reality is to think about the story you are creating for your child. Ask yourself what kind of story Kevote created initially for Spirit-Boy. Contrast this with the story Oscar's mother created for him. Understand that as a parent, you are like an author, crafting the structure for your child's life story with every choice you make. If you want the best for him, create his story from vision by beginning at the end.

A good writer envisions the story's ending and works backward to create the action that leads toward it. We have all read stories or seen movies with decent beginnings that fell apart in the middle or the end. If you don't want this to happen to your child, give him the best possible start by envisioning the adult he will become. Before I teach you how to do so, let me explain how I learned the importance of creating a life from vision.

If you had met me when I was in my twenties, you wouldn't recognize me today. Oh, I still look the same on the outside, plus a few pounds and wrinkles, but my heart and mind are different from that girl of long ago. When I was in my early twenties, I was a career-consumed young woman who traveled the globe and swore I would never settle down, get married or have children.

Yet, here I am today: the wife of a wise and caring man and the mother of two spirited and challenging little boys. The biggest surprise is that this adventure has been filled with such delight. If I compared the adventure of parenting to my globetrotting days, being a mother has been infinitely more intriguing and rewarding.

What I failed to realize in my twenties was that it wasn't a lack of desire that stopped me from wanting a family, but fear. Fear had stopped me from creating the one thing that has filled my heart the most.

What was I afraid of?

I was afraid of becoming like my parents.

Since I have realized that my fears are fairly common, I thought I'd share this story with you. My parents had a destructive relationship and I was terrified of sharing their destiny.

Since it was obvious to me that my parents didn't know how to create a happy life, I grew up without much respect for them and was afraid that if I had children, they would grow up disrespecting me. I didn't want to make all the sacrifices my parents grudgingly seemed to make only to raise children who disrespected or distrusted me.

The irony of this is that although I didn't trust my parents to give me the answers and traveled the globe in search of my own, in many ways, I ended up just like them. Even though I was unmarried and had no children, I was desperately unhappy. I didn't know how to have a loving relationship because I'd had no model for one. Worse yet, I lied to myself about how disenchanted and tortured I was.

Although I prided myself on being independent and different from my parents, I was walking a parallel path because, like them, I had created my life from Fear.

When Fear is your guiding force, it's impossible to create a joyful life. When Fear is the whisper in your ear that you heed most often, you've left your heart behind. I capitalize the word "fear" because in this culture, we deify it by letting it run and ruin our lives.

If you are creating your life from Fear, you are teaching your children to do the same. Those who are stuck in this intergenerational cycle of Fear are those whom the poet Thoreau described when he wrote, "The mass of men lead lives of quiet desperation." These are the people whose life decisions are guided primarily by what they fear.

One of the greatest gifts you can give your children is to break the cycle of Fear. In *Spirit-Boy and the Gift of Turquoise* (which appears in the Introduction to this book), when Kevote finally stops parenting from fear, she gives her son the freedom to discover his strengths, claim his nature and allow it to unfold. By investing Spirit-Boy with vision, rather than saddling him with fear, she encourages his awakening and facilitates her own. In doing so, she receives the sweetest gifts of all—the privilege of knowing her son's heart and the depths of her own.

The opposite of fear is vision. Vision is driven by love. The first step in breaking the cycle of fear is to go to the mirror and ask yourself some questions. Look yourself squarely in the eye and ask, "Do I love myself enough to create a joyful life?" Let your heart speak the answer to that question. Next, ask yourself, "Do I love my children enough to create a happy life, so I can show them what that looks like?" If you can't answer *yes!* for yourself, then answer for your children because as you learn to give them what you are secretly longing for, you will heal your broken heart.

Creating a life from vision, rather than fear is the first key to healthy parenting. Acting with vision breaks the cycle of Fear. The choice is as black and white as this—which do you choose for your children—a life of "quiet desperation" or a life of happiness? Although the answer should seem obvious, *ask yourself the question.* It is by failing to ask such questions in the first place that parents condemn their children to living lives of fear and disenchantment.

Choose right now. Get a journal and write on the very first page: "I choose to break the cycle of fear and teach myself and my children how to lead fulfilling lives." Sign and date it. This is your sacred promise to your children and yourself.

Children who grow up happy and healthy don't do so by accident. They do so because they have loving parents who model healthy relationships and make visionary choices for their future.

Creating a Vision for Your Child

The biggest mistake that Kevote makes in *Spirit Boy and the Gift of Turquoise* is that after her husband's death, she bases many of her decisions regarding Spirit-Boy on fear. Terrified of losing her son the way she lost her husband, she forbids him near the river. By focusing on what she fears, she creates it on a subtle level. She "loses" Spirit-Boy because she fails to know his heart. Instead of seeing who he is, she sees the traits that remind her of her husband. This angers Spirit-Boy because he feels invisible to the one person in the world whose love should make him feel *seen* and *whole*. When Spirit-Boy reaches the cusp of adolescence, Kevote has a choice: lose him forever or get to know his heart.

Although the river in the story may seem dangerous, it is an important symbol. In white society, we are uncomfortable with nature and the idea of following the heart, but the heart reveals the current of the soul. Although plunging into it may be risky to the ego, it is cleansing, invigorating and transforming. Since each of us must leap into the river to create a life to call our own, we must teach our children to respect the current and get their feet wet a little at a time.

To create a life from vision, you must listen to your heart. If I'd had the courage in my twenties to ask myself what I most wanted, it would have been a place where I belonged. I longed to surround myself with people who cherished and respected me and whom I cherished and respected in return. I wanted to *know* others, be known by them and give the gifts inside my heart. For me, that gift was writing. All my life, I have loved the music, truth and resonance of the written word.

But it's taken me most of my life to have the courage to believe that I had something of value to offer others.

Do I want this same painful struggle for my children? *Absolutely not.*

I want my children to take my hard won lessons and create their lives on a higher level. This is what good parenting and intergenerational evolution is all about.

How can I ensure that my children will have better lives than I had? By creating a vision for them, until they are old enough to create a vision of their own.

In his book, *Seven Habits for Highly Effective Families,* author Stephen Covey advises his readers to "begin with the end in mind." To parent with vision, the end is your starting point. This is in keeping with the Native American belief that humans must live from vision. A vision begins at its completion. Central to this belief is a practice called the Vision Quest.

The Vision Quest is a ritual that originated with native people. To Native Americans, the Vision Quest is a journey of self-discovery that awakens one's sense of purpose, meaning and relatedness with life. It is often performed in seclusion in the woods or desert where there are no distractions. This encourages the seeker to turn inward to find his purpose. Without food or shelter, the seeker is forced to rely on his inner knowing. This fosters self-confidence and initiates the transition from adolescence into adulthood.

Vision Quests are used for many reasons: to mark rites of passage, prepare for new roles and connect with or re-vision a sense of purpose. Although a child's first Vision Quest usually takes place during adolescence, Native Americans prepared their children for this event by teaching them survival skills and the ways of nature early on. The reason I advocate creating a vision for your child is that it makes parenting into a *practice* and lays the foundation for your child to create a vision of his own.

Before you can create a vision for your child, you'll need to have a vision of yourself. What kind of parent do you want to be? Remember my story about Oscar de la Hoya? In the end, the ultimate judge of your vision is your adult child. As an adult, what will he say about you? How will he say that you've contributed to the person he's grown to be?

Imagining such a scenario is not just a simple exercise, but a tool that will beckon the highest in you and give your parenting a sense of purpose, meaning and direction.

Before you begin, I'm going to ask you to add a crucial element to this exercise. Pretend that you are on your deathbed and your adult child is there with you, saying goodbye and thanking you for all you have given him.

Imagining your deathbed experience is an essential component of your vision because it forces you to acknowledge that children grow up quickly and some chances never come again. There's nothing worse than the deathbed regret of wishing that you had done more for those you love—especially your kids. There's nothing worse than realizing that you could have spent more time with them and loved them more fiercely and more fully.

In *American Indian Myths and Legends*, there is a Lakota story

26

about a young boy who goes into the woods on a Vision Quest. In his arrogance, the boy demands a vision that will make him into a great medicine man. The vision is not forthcoming. The boy returns to the village a failure, but learns a great lesson when his uncle tells him that "a vision comes as a gift of humility, of wisdom and of patience."

Imagining your deathbed experience creates the humility that allows you to peer deep inside your heart. Beginning at the end requires beginning at *your* end because your death provides the big perspective from which you must lead your life. This is in keeping with the native belief that the way to live from vision is to "remember your death."

Ready? Take a deep breath. Use your senses and imagine yourself on your deathbed. The room is comfortable. There is a vase of flowers on your nightstand. Their sweet, fading fragrance wafts past your nostrils, reminding you that your time is drawing near. Soon, you will leave this planet, surrounded by your family. One of your adult children takes your hand and choking back the tears, reflects upon all you have taught him. What in your heart of hearts, do you *long* to hear him say?

Listen inside yourself. Hear the words you yearn to hear. (You may hear a dialogue, get a feeling sense or see images. Work in whatever sensory mode best suits you. Trust yourself.) When you're finished, record what came to you in your journal.

If you need help with your deathbed vision, read my vision for my boys. If you use portions of it, make sure to make the words your own.

My heart would brim with happiness to hear my adult children say:

> *"I could always count on you to be there, mom. I could tell that you loved making our home a comfortable place filled with wonderful sights, smells and sounds. Because of this, I know that "home" should be a comforting place—a refuge— where I am surrounded by whom and what I cherish and where I can relax and be myself. Due to this experience, I carry "home" inside me everywhere where I go."*

> *"I could talk to you about what I was going through and*

you listened and helped me gain perspective. You saw inside me … you saw my strengths, even when I failed to see them myself. By encouraging me to follow them, you helped me to find my nature and develop the vision and self-discipline to walk the path toward my dreams."

"I could tell that you liked male company and enjoyed a healthy and loving relationship with my father, so I grew up respecting and trusting women and had an innate model for a good relationship. This is one reason I am able to have close relationships today. Your relationship with my father is the model for my loving and mutually supportive relationship with my wife."

"You taught me courage and conviction. You taught me to pick my battles wisely and to stand up for my beliefs."

"You taught me that there are some adults who don't have children's best interests in mind. You reminded me that it was your job to take issue with these people, so I could relax and be a kid. Due to this, I learned to trust myself, even in the face of adults who tried to manipulate or shame me. This taught me to know myself, so I wasn't tempted to blindly follow authority."

"You taught me how to listen because you listened attentively. You taught me openness because your heart and mind were open to my questions."

"You showed me that relationships matter more than things and that success is a measure of personal fulfillment. Because of this, I know that money is merely a byproduct of making my contributions to the world."

"You taught me to cherish life and walk gently on the Earth. You taught me that each thing in nature has a purpose, even though I might not know it. You showed me how to conserve

resources, so that my kids might enjoy the fruit and beauty of the Earth. You taught me to be thankful for the people in my life and the bounty of the planet."

"In respecting my development and that of those around you, you taught me to have humanity for others. You taught me to surround myself with those who show a willingness to grow."

"You taught me the value of being humble. You admitted your mistakes and showed me how apologies can be offered, lessons can be learned and wrongs can be amended. Due to this, I am forgiving with myself and others."

"You taught me to consider choices carefully because some decisions last forever."

"You taught me how to separate those who bring out the best in me from those who don't. Although this has helped me to create a close circle of supportive friends, it has also enabled me to choose not to invite certain people into my life."

"You taught me that true beauty radiates from the inside. I am not tricked by appearances because I know that outer beauty is not necessarily a reflection of what is in a person's heart."

"You taught me that it is what I give that makes me who I am. Things are just possessions. As a result of this, I know that my possessions don't define me."

"As I was growing up, I watched you grow as a person and a parent. This set a precedent for my growth and helped me to believe in its possibility."

"You are part of me, mom. I know that you and my dad have been the springboard to my becoming the person I am

today. While I honor and appreciate this, I know that your goal has always been to help me fully become myself. I know who I am. Since you had a vision for me, I have a vision for myself."

It's important to commit your words to paper. Once you do, you'll be able to define clearly what you want. More importantly, your hopes and dreams for your child will become a written contract with a greater aspect of yourself. In this way, your vision becomes a practice that guides your actions and defines how you raise your child.

Make sure to write the words as though your grown child were speaking to you, reflecting upon his childhood. Make certain that the scenario you imagine takes place on your deathbed. The power of this personal, heart-to-heart reflection will touch you in such a way that it will change your ideas about what it means to be a parent. This is what it is designed to do. Express what is in your heart. When you make your perspective big, yet personal, you give it a place of power in your life.

Let this vision guide you in your daily interactions with your child, even as it gently compares your behavior to your ideal. The gap between the parent you are and the parent you yearn to be will create positive momentum.

As time goes on, continue the process. Set aside some time to review your vision, make sure that you're aligned with it and revise it as needed. Use it as your *practice*—a means of guiding your behavior— and a reminder of what's truly important in your relationship with your child. When you forget, be gentle with yourself.

Qualities of a Visionary Mother and Father

A visionary parent lives in the present, while looking to the future and reflecting on the past. In between vision and reflection is conscious action. You're not a parent in the true sense of the word, unless you make your vision actionable. If you make promises, but fail to act on them, then your vision is nothing but a fantasy.

Let's stop for a moment and examine what defines a parent. In white American culture, a mother is someone who has given birth to a child. This title is bestowed upon her for one significant act: her ability to reproduce. It doesn't matter if she later abandons the child, she's still seen as his mother.

In other cultures, the word "mother" is viewed differently. My husband is a Pascua Yaqui Native American man and in his culture, the word "mother" is used as a verb. A mother is "one who mothers"— it is a title earned through action. Anyone, even a childless woman, can be a mother, provided she acts like one. In this way, native children have many mothers and mothers are honored for what they do.

Using "mother" as a verb is resourceful because it reinforces the importance of taking action. In this way, a mother's willingness to nurture is encouraged and acknowledged within the culture. By contrast, the use of "mother" as a noun creates a sense of obligation, dreary-drudging duty and for those who occasionally act the part, a strong sense of self-entitlement.

In *American Indian Myths and Legends,* there is teaching story from the Cochiti tribe about a neglectful mother. In the story, Crow is bored of sitting on her eggs and leaves the nest in search of an adventure. While she's gone, Hawk takes pity on the eggs and sits on them until they hatch. When Crow finally returns, she discovers that Hawk has been raising her chicks. Crow demands her babies back, but Hawk refuses, claiming *she* is their mother now. When an argument ensues, the King of Birds is called upon to decide their fate. The wise king asks the baby crows to identify their mother. The chicks point to Hawk. She is the one who has stayed with them and nurtured them from birth. Despite Crow's protests, the King of Birds decides that Hawk is the rightful mother of the chicks. The cultural message is clear: if you abandon your children, you give up your parental rights. A mother is one who mothers.

In the native world, "mothering" is intention expressed through action. It is a daily practice—a set of activities performed repeatedly toward mastery of a skill. A mother's skillfulness is reinforced each time her child calls her by name. Use this secret as a tool of inspiration. Each time your child calls you "mother," know that he is recognizing you for what you *do*. It doesn't matter whether his tone reveals this initially or not. If you act as though you're honored and respond with a genuine willingness to help, his respect and appreciation will grow. In this way, you become more responsive and your child facilitates your practice.

Of course, the same goes for fathers. A father is "one who fathers." You're not a father in the true sense of the word if all you've done is sow your seed. Through the father's guidance, the child-seed roots deeply into the earth and opens its newborn branches toward the sky.

Visionary parenting is about seeing what's not yet visible, yet taking steps toward it. This requires love, faith, creativity and patience. If you fear that you lack some of these qualities, let my words fall softly upon your ears and stir the courage in your heart. You are up to the task or you wouldn't have chosen this book.

As a caring mother or father, you'll turn your heartfelt wishes for your child into a plan of daily action. Since you probably haven't been a parent before (or if you have, you haven't raised this particular child before), realize that you don't have to do it perfectly and that your insights will allow you to make adjustments to the plan.

The beauty of parenting with vision is that it's mutually beneficial for both parent and child. Your child will grow up happy, strong, resilient and healthy and you will tap the wellspring of your heart. This is the essence of what I call "parent-child mutuality"—the "give and take" dance that fosters personal growth in child *and* parent, creating a relationship that nourishes and encourages both.

The Secrets of Making Your Vision into Reality

Using the underlying premise of parent-child mutuality, I've developed a four-step process to help you raise your child with vision and *without regrets*. This process is called E.A.R.A. Parenting and while the EAR in E.A.R.A. will remind you to use your senses and pay attention to what's happening around you, the individual letters stand for Envision, Action, Reflection and Adjustment.

E.A.R.A.'s four step process forms the basis of raising a happy, healthy child and will guide us into a new era of parenting. The first step is to **envision** your child as a happy, successful adult. Second, **act** in ways designed to make your vision come to be. Third, **reflect** upon how your plan is working and fourth, when appropriate, make **adjustments** to the plan.

At first glance, E.A.R.A. appears to be a circular process, but actually, it's a spiral. A circle is flat, while a spiral has dimension. As you envision, act, reflect and adjust your vision, you are evolving as a parent—maturing your ability to guide your child toward a better life, while honing your sense of parental purpose and responsibility.

E.A.R.A. engages you on all levels and helps you to become a visionary, responsive, reflective and resilient parent. These are the qualities that you'll need to raise a child who is happy and healthy and with whom you'll share a lifetime relationship of mutual love, honor and respect. One benefit is that you will become a better human being in the process.

If you need help with these ideas, a workbook/journal is available exclusively from my web site: www.parenting-child-development.com. The downloadable workbook breaks these concepts into concrete, actionable steps. It will help you make these teachings part of your life.

Whether or not you purchase the workbook, I encourage you to use E.A.R.A. technology: envision what you most want for your child, act with those goals in mind and reflect upon what your actions have created. As you grow along with your child, you will make adjustments that reflect a refined understanding of what your child needs from you and a growing desire to give him the best life has to offer.

The Oracle of the Child

In E.A.R.A. parenting, the ability to reflect upon your plan and make adjustments is an important skill. Although many parents will recognize that ineffective strategies must be re-visioned, if you want a different take on how you're doing as a parent, ask your child. Since children are honest, make sure you really want to know. Parents make a big mistake when they ask their child a pointed question and then fail to listen or get angry because the answer given is not what they had hoped to hear. If you do this often, then your child will refuse to answer or tell you only what you want to hear. This is one way parents train their children to be dishonest.

Although your child may not be able to fully express himself, realize that in his answer is a kernel of the truth. That kernel may be something you need to work on or something that your child needs from your relationship, but isn't getting. In your journal, record your child's words, but assign no meaning to them, unless you immediately recognize what he's trying to say. Let the deeper answer come to you in "Aha!" moments of quiet reflection, before falling asleep, while in the shower or upon awakening. Often children speak in a language that we think we understand, until we open ourselves to looking at the world through their eyes.

I regularly ask my children how I'm doing as a mother. When they answer, I listen attentively. I ask them if they feel respected. I ask them if they think the rules are just and designed for their protection and growth as human beings. I ask them if they feel cherished. I ask them if they believe that I see into their hearts. I ask them if there's anything they need that I'm not giving them. I initiate these talks during the quiet moments following a family dinner, on the drive home from school or just before they fall asleep. Their answers are always thoughtful and respectful.

During one of these conversations, my eldest son, Dakotah, made an observation that I've held dear and used as a guiding principle ever since. He said, "Mom, one thing I can tell about you is that you really like us kids and are interested in our lives."

To have my son recognize the difference between love and like touched me deeply. While many parents believe it is their duty to love their children, some parents dislike their kids, although they would never admit it. Such parents go through the motions and act the part, but on some level, their children sense the truth.

A child who is liked by her parents grows up liking herself and understands the gift of interest. Children know the difference between parents who go through the motions because they're afraid of what others think and those who consistently act in the children's highest good because they love and genuinely *like* their kids. This is the difference between doing your duty and acting from the heart.

Although your children may not initially have something positive to say, the point is to start an open dialogue. If your child says something hurtful, investigate why it offends you and whether it is true or even partially true. This is a time in which you allow your child to hold a mirror to you. Summoning the courage to look into your child's eyes and see your reflection will tell you what you need to learn to become a better parent.

If your child understands that the rules ensure his safety and foster his growth into a caring human being, he will not question them because they will be reasonable. Creating a space for open dialogue does not mean that parental rules are open for negotiation. It means that you are open to learning and making adjustments when you discover that you have been rigid. Open discussion creates a foundation of mutual respect and honesty that will become the basis of your relationship.

How Fears Conflict with Vision

We opened this chapter with fear and we are going to close with it. Of all a parent's deficits, fear is probably the biggest stumbling block in helping a sacred vision come to be. As an adult, you've probably realized how your parents' fears have shaped you and know that they will shape your child unless *you* change. To do so, you must understand how fear tricks you and prevents you from becoming who you are.

In general, people are motivated either by love or fear. If you want the best for your child, then you'll want him to heed what's in his heart, rather than zig-zagging anxiously through life as though it were a minefield. In this way, your child's life becomes one of intention, rather than avoidance. Like Kevote in *Spirit-Boy and the Gift of Turquoise*, in order to teach your child how to live a life of vision, you must take an honest look at how often your decisions are distorted by your fears.

Take a close look at your life. How have you come by your achievements? Have you obtained them by avoiding what you're afraid of or by creating what's in your heart? Be careful here because the answer can be tricky. Having wealth and power doesn't mean you aren't a fear-based person. Nor does it mean you are. And being a starving artist doesn't necessarily mean that you are following your heart. Probe beyond stereotypes and peer unblinkingly into your life.

Although this isn't a book about helping you overcome your fears, in order to carry out your sacred vision, you must be honest about how you operate. If you're primarily a fear-based person, then admit this to yourself. By acknowledging your fears, you'll loosen their chokehold.

If you deny your fears, then you unwittingly pass them to your children. In doing so, you condemn them to live your life, which is not what they are here to do.

To illustrate how fears are passed between generations, allow me to share an example from my life. As I mentioned earlier, my parents operated primarily from fear. Compounding this, was the fact that my father was in and out of work and was always changing jobs. This meant we moved constantly, often out-of-state.

Although I didn't realize it yet, my parents' fears and the upheaval caused by constant moving made me terrified of change. It wasn't until I was in my thirties and my husband had a heart attack that I began to get a glimmer of how much I operate from fear. At the time, my husband was the sole breadwinner and our boys were two and four. Adding to my fears were these realities: my husband is handicapped (the result of a major car accident), lives with spinal cord pain, is diabetic and travels out-of-state to work.

After my husband's heart attack, I was besieged by "what if" scenarios. Rather than wait and see if these "what ifs" actually occurred, I acted *as though they had*. I was convinced that my husband would be unable to work and I would have to support the family, despite growing evidence to the contrary.

After considering several options, I decided to build an online store. This way, I could contribute to the family income, while staying home, helping my husband recover and raising our two boys. Since I knew nothing about building an online business, I read books about web design, copy writing, graphic design and marketing. I built a business called Kokopelli's Treasures that featured southwestern style lighting and home décor.

Due to a limited budget, I did everything myself: I was the webmaster, graphic designer, photographer, search engine expert, copywriter, marketer, accountant, buyer, shipper and receiver. I even obtained a trademark.

For the first two years, I ran my business at home and had a hard time closing the office door. Wanting to be an attentive mother and wife and spend time with my family, I woke up as early as 4:00 a.m. and went to bed long after everyone else had gone to sleep, so I could get my work done. I did laundry between business calls, cooked while I took orders, helped my kids with their homework and drove them to their sporting events and lessons. Although I'd built this business so I could contribute to the family income after my husband's heart attack, I was headed straight for a heart attack of my own.

I never had that heart attack, but eventually, things came to a head because I couldn't continue to do it all anymore. In addition to running the web site, taking care of the house and kids and helping my husband recover from the emergency triple bypass that he eventually had to have, I was writing and publishing a monthly online parenting newsletter called *Family Matters*. In other words, I was the quintessential woman-who-does-too-much.

Since I spent my time rushing from one task to the next, I had no time for self-reflection, which is why I couldn't see the way out of my self-created trap.

Although building a business might have seemed sensible in light of my husband's health problems, I had fallen into an old routine. Instead of responding to the situation at hand, I reacted by preparing for the worst.

Preparing for the worst is a war-and-poverty mentality construct. It's what I call the Armageddon Syndrome. It's a frenzied preparation for what you view to be the ultimate showdown between good and evil, between the worst "what if" forces in the universe and you. Preparing for the worst is what people do when they have lost their faith or never had it in the first place.

Since you don't believe that the universe will support you or that your circumstances hold a valuable lesson for your growth, you're convinced that you have to do everything to prepare for the realization of your greatest fears. You scurry around like a crazy person, collecting rations, hoarding pennies and securing the fort, while completely ignoring the fact that the enemy isn't banging down your door.

Although there's nothing wrong with being prepared, there's a big difference between planning for the future and preparing for the worst. Preparing for the worst means that on some level, you expect it. When you *expect* something horrible, you become pregnant with its possibility. In this way, preparing for the worst can be a self-fulfilling prophecy. Despite this, our greatest fears are seldom realized.

What does this story have to do with parenting?

Absolutely everything.

Like Kevote in *Spirit-Boy and the Gift of Turquoise*, you can't teach your children how to live from vision if you live from fear. Reflecting upon the ways in which you act from fear is the first step in preventing your children from functioning as you have.

Although creating from fear means that you'll end up with a life that is an expression of those fears, there is much that you can gain from this experience. When I think about the business that I built from fear, I also have to acknowledge that it was balanced by my passions. I love the symbolism of Native American art and southwestern style décor. Having an e-commerce site involved writing, art and photography, which I enjoy. Since most of the items that I sold were artist made, I had the honor of promoting unknown artisans.

Building a successful business required that I learn subjects in which I had not been schooled and for which I had little affinity: accounting, management, marketing, advertising, web site design, order fulfillment, etc. Since I had little interest in these things, learning them required grit and determination. Best of all, the experience of realizing what I no longer want—to operate from fear—has deepened my commitment to following my heart.

When I look back at all that I've learned in the past three years, I'm astounded. I look at what I created from fear and wonder what I could create with love. This book is a product of my curiosity.

What can *you* create with love?

If you've never asked yourself this question, now is the time to ask. Even if you haven't found your calling in life, you've given birth to someone you love dearly or you wouldn't be reading this book.

If you do nothing in life out of the ordinary, raising your children with vision will make you into an extraordinary human being. Looking into your children's heart will help you see into your own.

Believe in love. Believe in children and their future. Not just your children: all the children of the world. Show your faith by using your vision to aspire to be the best parent you can be and create a skillful beginning for your child's life story. Acknowledge your fears and make living from vision your daily practice.

Chapter 2

Embracing Your Sacred Role as Guardian

You are your child's keeper, until she's ready to keep herself.

Becoming Your Child's Keeper

Your child does not belong to you, but she is yours *to keep*. This statement reveals the distinction between guardianship and ownership. Your child is "yours to keep" because you are her *keeper*—the guardian of her body, mind and spirit. You are "keeping" her, until she's ready to "keep" herself.

What is a keeper? A keeper is the caretaker of something rare, be it an estate, a priceless gem or an ancient book of wisdom. You have the privilege of being the keeper of something infinitely more precious—the keeper of a child. If you are a parent who focuses on all the perceived sacrifices of parenting, then you are missing the miracle that is unfolding right before your eyes.

As a parent, what do you keep? You keep your child's heart, mind, spirit, body, future, trust, ideals, values, beliefs and self-perceptions. You are your child's keeper until he's ready to become the custodian of his life. As that moment gradually approaches, you'll slowly release your hold on him and if you've done your job properly, he will become the keeper of his life.

Creating Good Medicine

In Chapter 1, I asked you to write a vision that defines what you most want for your child. As a parent, you are the keeper of this sacred vision. Your vision is more than just a written contract, just as your role as guardian involves more than tending to your child's physical needs.

Many parents falsely believe that if they feed, clothe and shelter their child, they're doing enough. This is one aspect of guardianship that has to do with taking care of physical needs. In *Spirit-Boy and the Gift of Turquoise*, when Old Eyes points out that Kevote feeds her child, but starves his spirit, she means that Spirit-Boy has emotional and spiritual needs that must be tended too. Of course, in the hierarchy of human needs, the physical is first.

By envisioning your child as a happy and successful adult, you've committed to providing more than just the physical. Although tending your child's physical needs is crucial to her development, her other needs are equally important.

Take a moment and look back over your vision again. What is the common thread that connects your highest wishes for your child?

Reflecting upon my vision, I see that my ultimate hope for my children is that they will grow up knowing how to create fulfilling lives. I want them to know who they are, what they yearn for and have the heart to work toward their dreams. I want to teach them how to *thrive* and lead lives that bring them meaning and fulfillment. This is my directive as a parent.

Teaching your children how to live good lives is what Native Americans call creating "good medicine." Good medicine cultivates the energy to build a healthy body, mind and spirit because it speaks the language of the heart. Good medicine heals old wounds. A daily dose will help your children ward off diseases of the mind and spirit, such as "quiet desperation," which rob the heart of the courage to seek its way.

What constitutes "good medicine" for one may be different for another. This is best illustrated by a children's story I wrote called *How Coyote and Beaver Became Good Friends*. In the story, soon after Coyote meets Beaver, Beaver takes ill. Wanting to be a good friend, Coyote invites Beaver to his den, so he can nurse him back to health. Knowing that Beaver must eat to get well, Coyote brings him a mouse, but Beaver turns up his nose at it. Next Coyote catches a rabbit, but Beaver isn't interested. At first, Coyote is offended, but then tries to figure out what other kind of food to bring his friend. Since Beaver lives in the pond, Coyote figures he must eat fish. After quite a struggle, Coyote catches one, but Beaver refuses it as well. Coyote fumes, but later that evening when he hears Beaver moaning in his sleep, he resolves to try again. The next day, when Beaver refuses the water that Coyote brings him from the pond, he realizes his friend is dying. He paces outside his den, looking for an answer. He eyes Beaver's watery dam, thinks about his warm, dry den and realizes how different he is from his friend. Knowing that most animals live near their food source, he carefully surveys the pond, but all he sees are a tangle of willows growing by the water's edge. He can't believe that Beaver would eat something as unappetizing as branches, but figures it's worth a shot. He breaks off one and passes it before Beaver's nose. His nostrils quiver. While Coyote holds one end of the branch between his teeth, Beaver gnaws weakly at the other end. As the days pass, he steadily regains his strength. When he has fully recovered, he tenderly scratches a hard-to-reach spot on Coyote's back that has been bothering him. Coyote and Beaver have become good friends and "bringers of good medicine." Beaver slides into the water and paddles home.

This story illustrates that what is "good medicine" for one may be ineffective or even harmful to another. People can't give good medicine if they are unable to separate their needs from those of others. To dispense good medicine, you must be able to see into another's heart and give them what they need. The most concrete illustration of this comes from the animal world: coyotes prey on animals, but beavers get their nourishment from bark. When Coyote finally grasps that Beaver is different from him, he figures out how to minister to his needs. Good medicine is more than food—it is the sense of *comfort* Beaver feels when Coyote sees his nature. The original meaning of *comfort* is "to strengthen." Coyote's recognition gives Beaver the strength to journey home.

To learn how to give your child good medicine, you must learn to speak the language of his heart. We will discuss this further in Chapter 3. For now, realize that although few parents purposely raise their children to lead lives of quiet desperation, the parent who raises her child without taking the time to know his heart may discover that she unwittingly led him straight down this path. Imagine how you would feel if one day, you realized how you had helped create the life of your angry, dispirited or drug-addicted teenage or adult child.

Like Kevote in *Spirit-Boy and the Gift of Turquoise*, when you encourage what's in your child's heart, you give good medicine. Good medicine lifts your child's spirits and gives him the courage to know himself, develop and own his strengths. Good medicine is the gateway to self-knowledge and fulfillment.

41

What better gift can you give your child than the tools to create a fulfilling life? If you focus your energy on showing your child how to use these tools, you will raise a child who honors, cherishes and respects you because you have taught him the secrets of genuine happiness.

Becoming a Worthy Guardian

In order to raise a child who will cherish, honor and respect you, you must become a worthy guardian. How does a worthy guardian behave? Think about your childhood for a moment. Were you fortunate enough to have a true guardian in your life? If you were and if this person happened to be one or both your parents, then you had role models, who taught you how to know and guide yourself.

If you weren't blessed with such a parent, then perhaps you have encountered an angel once or twice. Angels appear in human form with the perfect words to help you see what's right before your eyes. An angel can be a friend who finally blurts out the one truth that you didn't want to hear (but needed to) or a stranger who nudges you in a way that enables you to do something that you couldn't do before. An angel initiates a wake-up call by urging you to rub the sleep from your eyes and see a higher truth.

The difference between an angel and a guardian is that an angel touches you momentarily, while a guardian is a constant in your life. Think of a guardian as an everyday angel. Although "everyday" implies ordinary or mundane, a guardian is nothing less than extraordinary.

Keeping the Sacred Trust

Trust is the foundation of any relationship, but it is especially crucial between a child and parent. The parent-child bond is the model for every relationship that follows it. Your child's level of trust in you colors her expectations and perceptions of everyone who comes into her life.

When a child puts his trust in you, you must act in ways that honor it. Since a baby is helpless and has no choice but to trust you, you are responsible for earning his trust the moment he is born. Actually, trust begins in the womb. It begins with a mother's unspoken promise that she will nurture her body and give her fetus the best possible start.

Trust is so essential that the great analyst, Erik Erikson, defined it as a crucial element in the first stage of human development. Erikson called this stage *trust vs. mistrust.* During this stage, a child's experience of his caretakers (as responsive and consistent or unresponsive and unreliable) creates the template for future relationships with others.

The problem is that although we operate continually from a base of trust or mistrust, we're unaware of it. Trust or mistrust is like a lens through which we view the world. Because the lens was formed before we were capable of reasoning, we are unaware that we have our glasses on.

When facing the unknown or meeting someone new, the issue of *trust vs. mistrust* surfaces again. This is why Erikson called his stages "life cycles"—because the trust issue continues to arise, until we become aware of how it primes our perceptions. By understanding how your early experiences created this overlay, you can begin to peel it off, giving yourself a choice and giving the people in your life a chance to show you that they may be different from your parents.

This illustrates why children's experiences with primary caregivers are so profound—they set the stage for all the acts to follow.

The Facets of Trust

Now that we've underscored the importance of trust, let's explore its meaning. In *The New World Dictionary*, trust is defined as "a firm belief or confidence in the honesty, integrity, reliability and justice of another."

Let's take these elements and break them down. First is honesty, which means telling the truth. Since truth telling can be used to heal or wound, watch the intention behind your words. Always temper the truth with kindness, particularly when dealing with a child. Since there are some truths that your child is not ready for, offer concrete details only when necessary and appropriate.

Even a fairly truthful parent can get trapped in telling lies, especially when it's a lie that's perpetuated by culture. For instance, what have you told your children about Santa Claus? When my children were little, I told them that Santa was a man who dressed in costume to remind us of the importance of giving. When I shared this story with an acquaintance, she said that she had never told her kids that Santa was real, but hadn't told them that he *wasn't* real either. She didn't understand that children are concrete and when you take them to see Santa Claus and sit them in his lap, they believe that he exists as a real person in the world. When viewed from a child's perspective, a lie of omission is no different than a lie of commission.

Although I was only five when I discovered that Santa did not exist, I still remember how betrayed I felt. I recall it as *the* moment when I began to question everything my parents and other adults said. Even as a little girl I sensed that Santa had been used to coerce my good behavior.

Although some parents claim that they use Santa Claus as a way to teach the joy of giving, many of these same parents use Christmas gifts as a means to threaten or bribe their children. This brings to mind a song from childhood—*I'm Getting' Nuttin' for Christmas*—in which a boy laments that he's getting no Christmas gifts because he's been "nuttin' but bad." If parents believe that Christmas is about teaching the spirit of giving, then gifts must not be contingent on good behavior. As caring parents, we must use cultural myths as they were intended—to engage our children's imaginations in a playful, non-manipulative way that teaches and inspires them.

Unfortunately, I've seen some parents take the Santa Claus thing to extremes. For instance, the parents who hand over their screaming toddler to the mall Santa just to get a photograph for their scrapbook are committing an act that borders on abuse. Santa is scary looking—a big male with a long white beard and after all, he *is* a stranger. It makes perfect sense for children to be afraid of him.

Another common lie is the this-won't-hurt-you lie. Medical professionals often tell this lie when administering a shot. If a nurse says this to your child, counter her statement by preparing your child for what he will experience. You can say, "Shots *do* hurt. It feels like a pinch or sting, but it stops hurting after a couple of minutes. The shot is necessary because it will prevent you from getting a disease that will hurt you more."

When my children need to have a shot, my husband and I tell them to pinch themselves, while the shot is being administered. If your children have some sense of controlling the pain, then the shot will seem to hurt less. Teaching your child this little secret is a caring way to build his trust in you when he's feeling vulnerable.

While it's an art to prepare your child for reality without terrifying him, you can help by being truthful and explaining experiences in terms of concrete sensations. If you're unfamiliar with the sensations, try it first yourself. If it's a medical procedure that you cannot simulate, then talk to someone who has gone through it, so you'll have a good idea of how your child may feel before, during and after.

The next aspect of trust is integrity. Integrity implies wholeness and sameness. This means that your words and deeds must arise from a consistent set of values. We'll be discussing the importance of your words a little later. For now, make sure to choose words carefully and remember that to children, they are promises that must be kept.

The next part of trust is reliability, which implies dependability and sameness. You must be a person on whom your child can depend. You must also be a consistent presence. A child needs a parent who is there for the daily struggles, not a "sometimer" or weekend mom or dad. If you can't always be there physically, then be present through other means, such as daily conversations on the phone. Remember that your child relies on you for many things: physical safety, emotional comfort and spiritual guidance.

Justice is the final aspect of our definition of trust. As defined by the *New World Dictionary,* justice is "the authority to uphold what is right." Be thoughtful about what you define as "right." Rightness should arise from vision that's tempered by an understanding of your child's current level of development.

When dealing with a group of children, think about what my husband once said: "Justice isn't for "*just us,*" but for "*us all.*" Although many lawyers think of justice as an umbrella that only covers some, refuse to buy into this convenient definition. By finding a deeper sense of justice, which embraces the best interests of *children as a whole,* you teach your child that he is part of something bigger than himself.

Trust and Privilege

Although your child has no choice but to trust you at birth, treat his faith in you as an honoring. By giving you his trust, he is passing you a sparkling gem of which you are the keeper. Polish it with your sense of honesty, integrity, reliability and justice, then give it back. Every time this exchange occurs, your child's trust in you will deepen.

As your child grows, use the gem of trust as a metaphor for your relationship. Invest your trust in your child and he will give it back. I do this with my kids by telling them little things that I expect them to keep within the family. When I tell them things that aren't meant for others' ears, rather than spell it out, I say the code words: "Sacred Gem of Trust."

I often do this with insights into other people's character that will help illustrate a lesson or teach our children to make better choices than authorities or friends. If these observations were shared with someone outside the family, that person might perceive them to be hurtful. While I want my children to see how people reveal their character through action, I don't want them sharing these judgments with people who may be unequipped to handle them. The intention is not to hurt or analyze anyone, but to create a strong family identity based on humane values and to assist my children in making healthy choices about whom to choose as friends and role models.

While you will expect your child to keep your confidences, remember that the Sacred Gem of Trust works both ways—you must also keep the secrets with which you have been entrusted.

One day, when your child has many choices about whom to trust, he will freely place his trust in you. Right now, because he's naïve and dependent, he has no choice. Since he'll learn the sanctity of the sacred gem through your exchanges and the ways in which you place your trust in him, he will become its keeper.

It is a glorious moment in parenting when you witness your child acting with honesty, integrity, reliability and justice on his own. There's no reward more fitting for a parent who has given her child the tools he needs to act in ways that are congruent with deeply cherished values.

The I-Thou Relationship

The parent-child relationship is sacred. Many parents are neglectful of their sacred duties not because they don't care, but because they lack a model for the inner workings of a healthy parent-child relationship. Since many parents didn't have attentive, conscientious parents, they don't know how to influence their children positively without raising them to be spoiled.

In 1923, as part of his *Philosophy of Dialogue*, theologian Martin Buber described what he called the I-Thou relationship. Such a relationship is based on mutuality, openness and directness. The I-Thou relationship creates a genuine dialogue between two people in which one sees and encourages the individuality of the other. In this relationship, the parent is "I" and the child is "Thou."

Thou is an address of familiarity which has been replaced by the pronoun "you." Using *thou* in reference to your child indicates that you know him. But *thou* is also short for thousand. When we combine these meanings, we describe the essence of a healthy parent-child relationship. A parent who practices an I-Thou relationship with her child knows her child is unique and multi-faceted. Each characteristic of a child is an aspect of the whole.

In the native world, the I-Thou relationship describes man's relationship with Nature. Native Americans believe that Nature is equivalent to God. In this way, the "thou" are the many guises that the Creator wears—from a blade of grass to a redwood tree, from a gnat to a buffalo—everything is enervated by God's presence. To Native Americans, the Earth is sacred. Plants and animals are brothers because it is our relatedness with all of life—the "I" in conjunction with the "Thou"—which sustains us and gives life meaning.

The I-Thou relationship is sacred. Like Native Americans, Buber described it in terms of man's relationship with God. This is different from what he referred to as the I-It relationship in which the participants are unequal. While an I-It relationship may lead to knowledge, the I-Thou relationship creates wisdom and self-awareness in relation to the whole. In the relationship between child and parent, the child learns who he is first through his parents and finally, gains self-insight through experience and reflection. Since the I-Thou relationship is one of mutuality, the give-and-take dance between parent and child fosters greater awareness in both. This calls to mind the age-old question: who is teacher and who is student? The answer is *each* and *both*.

In our culture, the focus on information has led to the pursuit of objective knowledge. This I-It focus has permeated every aspect of our existence, including how we raise and school our children, especially with regard to the current strategy of teaching-for-the-tests.

In the following sections, you'll begin to see how cultivating an I-Thou relationship with your child will do more than meet your child's dependency needs. It will teach him *how to thrive*.

The Seeker and the Sage

Although the I-Thou relationship has been applied successfully to the therapeutic setting, I am unaware of any book that describes its use in parenting. In this section, I'll illustrate why the I-Thou relationship is the cornerstone of parenting and how in many ways, your relationship with your child parallels that of the seeker and the sage.

Entering into an I-Thou relationship with your child means that you see your child as your spiritual equal. Before someone uses this idea to justify an extreme form of parental permissiveness, let me emphasize that although your child is your spiritual equal, he is not your equal in self-knowledge, maturity or the workings of the world. Due to this, you must act as a protector and guide by defining the limits and teaching your child how to make healthy choices.

As a facilitator of the I-Thou relationship, your role is many faceted. You must be an authority and guide, even as you allow yourself to be a student. Like your child, you are learning. You are learning how to be a parent, to counsel, to see and bring forth the light that is in your child. As you are learning how to parent, your child is learning to see and know himself, to understand how the world works and how to create a place in it. Acknowledging that you are walking the path of learning will help you develop patience and empathy for yourself and your child.

The essence of the I-Thou relationship is in creating an authentic connection with your child. Since you've "been there and done that," you can offer empathy and guidance for all the stages through which your child must pass on the way to becoming an adult.

It takes a *mature* adult to raise a child to maturity. The I-Thou relationship facilitates this because it is based on respect for and empowerment of the other.

Since the I-Thou relationship is based on mutuality, it cultivates the twin seed—the seed of your child's *becoming* and your growth into a mature human being.

The Privilege of Parent-Child Intimacy

Cultivating the I-Thou relationship creates enduring intimacy. Since many people use the word "intimate" in reference to sexuality, let's rediscover its broader meaning and application to parenthood. When you're intimate with a child, you know his heart, mind and nature. This grants you passage into his private world.

Intimacy is a privilege of parenting. With this privilege comes the opportunity to witness the blossoming of a unique heart and mind.

In the beginning of your relationship, you are the center of your child's universe. Like the sun, you provide warmth and sustenance. Like God, you are the seer, the omnipotent judge and mighty protector. Unfortunately, many parents abuse this power because they see it as their right, rather than as their *privilege*.

When considering how to wield your power gently, remember that during the early years, your right of presence goes unquestioned. Although you are given access to your child's private world initially, as he matures, your privileges can be revoked.

When parents find that their "rights" have been denied, they may demand them back, forcing entry into their child's private world. This makes them intruders, rather than welcome guests.

Intimacy is a privilege. Although you endured thirty-six hours of labor to give birth to this child and you work yourself to the bone to provide for her, this doesn't give you the right to emotional or spiritual intimacy. You are granted the privilege of intimacy by earning it through continual expressions of love, interest, responsiveness and your commitment to knowing your child's heart.

The Compassionate Witness

In her writings about abused children, psychologist Alice Miller, talks about the value of the "compassionate witness." A compassionate witness is someone who reads between the lines to acknowledge what another is going through.

In a neglected or abused child's life, the acknowledgment of a compassionate witness is good medicine and can mean the difference between a child thinking that she's crazy and knowing that she's not. While other adults in the child's life may be in denial, a compassionate witness sees the truth. A compassionate witness is often the reason why two children can suffer the same trauma and while the one without a witness may be scarred forever, the one with a compassionate witness emerges with a stronger sense of self.

While a compassionate witness is not always able to stop what's happening to a child, by acknowledging reality, the witness makes the child feel that she's not alone in her perceptions. What's happening *is* happening and it is wrong. A compassionate witness can be a parent, grandparent, teacher, friend, neighbor or anyone who confirms the truth of a child's suffering.

For instance, let's say that Billy, an eight-year-old boy, has a father who's an alcoholic. His father's drinking brings out his cruelty, but no one in the family has the courage to confront him. Billy's mother cowers when her drunken husband beats the boy for minor things. Billy's father has been drinking for years and because of this, Billy thinks his home life and his father's behavior is "normal," even though his heart stops whenever he hears his father uncap a beer. One day, Billy has a friend over named Allen, who watches as Billy's drunken father berates him. The next day, Billy comes to school with a black eye. Allen puts his arm around Billy and takes a leap, "Things are tough at home, huh? I know what that's like. I used to have a stepfather, who'd get drunk and hit me, but my mom finally kicked him out."

Even though Billy may have no hope of his mother ever confronting his father, he breathes a sigh of relief because now he has a compassionate witness of his home life. Without actually saying that Billy's father is an alcoholic, Allen has acknowledged that Billy's suffering is real. From what Allen has said, Billy also knows that his mother should stand up for him. Even though he knows this only by inference, Billy knows now that he's not crazy. His parents are the crazy ones. Although Billy's situation may not change, Allen has opened up a window in Billy's mind from which he can breathe fresh air when things get stifling at home again.

As a parent, you can be a compassionate witness for your child. You can do this at home, at school or out in the world. For instance, if your husband lashes out at your children, it's helpful to take your children aside and say that their daddy's having a bad day and probably didn't mean to hurt their feelings. Of course, when your husband realizes that he's overreacted, he should apologize.

With regard to things that happen at school, I act as a compassionate witness for my children all the time. As we drive home from school, I ask them about their day. When one of my children feels that he was treated unjustly by a friend or teacher, I listen attentively to his story. Active listening is good medicine. When a child's troubles are met by receptive ears, his posture straightens and his resiliency returns. A child who is listened to feels *seen* and *heard*. If something has happened at school that requires my intervention, I take a stand.

For instance, on several occasions, I've taken a stand against the elementary school's policy of zero tolerance. Zero tolerance means that a school will not tolerate violence and will punish everyone involved in a conflict. To me, zero tolerance is like Nancy's Reagan's anti-drug campaign: "Just Say, No." Although it makes a catchy slogan, it fails to address the source of the problem. People who can say "no" to drugs are not those who have the problem.

In a similar fashion, zero tolerance seeks to prevent violence by punishing everyone involved. Not only does this fail to resolve the conflict, it is lazy (since everyone is punished, the authorities don't need to take the time to sort things out) and in many cases, it is unjust. My son was once given a detention simply for blocking another child's punches. As a compassionate witness, I challenged the detention and supported my son for refusing to be a victim.

Educators must take a closer look at the message that policies like zero tolerance send. When bullies and victims are treated the same, children learn that there is no difference between the two. Why be a victim, when the penalty for being a bully is the same? In this way, a policy designed to prevent violence actually promotes it.

Where there is zero tolerance, there can be no sense of restorative justice or closure. In terms of teaching children emotional intelligence skills, it is a missed opportunity.

At home, you can be a compassionate witness for your children's friends. Although some kids might seem unapproachable, by inviting them to your home and letting them see how the members of a loving family interact, you offer them a different take on family life. The contrast will show them that abuse is not okay and does not equal love or security. This is good medicine to carry with them back into their lives.

Being a compassionate witness means becoming a guardian of *the* children. When you realize your role as guardian, the distinction between *my* children and *your* children falls away. Being a compassionate witness of the children means opening your heart to the innocent, who have less experience and power of choice than you. This is the true meaning of stewardship.

The Guardian Watch

As a guardian, you're responsible for keeping a watchful eye on the other guardians in your child's life. Since your child spends at least six hours a day at school, it is your job to know the school policies, understand the reasoning behind them and be aware of how they are carried out.

Before we continue, let's define the meaning of responsibility. Responsibility literally means "response-ability:" or the ability to respond. We all have this ability, yet many parents fail to act, even when they know they should. The actions we should have taken—but didn't—often turn into lifelong regrets.

In this book, we'll use the word responsibility to mean *the preparedness and willingness to act and follow through.*

The first step of response-ability is preparation. The only way to be prepared is to know what's going on. This requires that you watch, listen and learn. It means that when you pick up your children from school, you ask general and then pointed questions about what happened during their day. Rather than grilling them, establish an open or "I-Thou" dialogue that shows your children that they can trust you and that you are interested in their lives. Being prepared also means getting to know your child's teacher and other school authorities. You can do this through volunteer work at the school.

The second part of response-ability is a willingness to act. In order to do so, you must overcome any residual fear of authority figures.

If the thought of meeting with the school principal makes your heart race, then you need to work through your fears (or act in spite of them) for the benefit of your child.

When I talk about the willingness to act, I'm referring to responding, rather than reacting. Reacting implies action without thought. It often means acting from a place of righteous indignation, which makes resolution impossible because both parties perceive that they are under attack. While in some cases, a threat may be the only way to make an impact, I prefer to start out by gathering facts and illustrating to school authorities how certain policies can lead to dangerous outcomes at the school.

As the parent of elementary school children, I have been surprised at some of the things that have happened at our school. Keep in mind that this is a school with less than five hundred students, a low teacher-student ratio and few incidents of violence. While most school authorities are thoughtful, committed and caring, I've been stunned by the behavior of a few that reveal little understanding of child development and a lack of vision. I've seen policies designed primarily to protect the school from lawsuits, rather than protect the children and methods that reveal an underlying belief that children have no rights. Of course, most of these policies are designed by the school board and principals and teachers are required to follow them.

When something happens at school that I strongly disagree with, I go in and present my case. Apparently, few parents do this. In fact, many parents believe that the school system is above reproach. I learned this when I received a heated email response to an article I wrote on zero tolerance. In this email, a parent wrote, "When you send your children to school, you abdicate your authority to the school." Although I was a bit surprised by this response, it made sense later when I learned that this woman was both a parent and a teacher.

Since that time, I've found out that other parents share this belief. They accept what happens at their children's school, even though they may disagree with it. When parents complain to me about something that has happened at school, I advise them to talk to the teacher or principal. More often than not, the parent replies, "But ... I don't want to make waves."

If you don't want to "rock the boat," when the rocking the boat will create forward movement, then you must examine your residual fears of authority. Many parents shrink in the face of school authorities, as though principals and teachers still control them. If this sounds familiar, then it's time to gently remind yourself that you're a tax-paying adult and that the principal, teachers and school counselors are county employees who *work for you.* In addition to working for you, they must work for the children by protecting them and serving the highest good of children as a whole.

As an adult, you need to recognize that like children, we are all in the process of learning. No one can possibly know everything. As parents, we are responsible for helping other adults become aware of the things that we've observed and the policies and procedures that may need to be refined. If you approach adults with kindness and regard, they will show interest in your observations and a willingness to consider them. Of course, some authorities will be offended or indifferent, which means that you will have to go above their heads.

If an authority at your child's school demeans or humiliates your child, it's up to you to take a stand. Children count on parents to fight the battles in the adult world, so they can concentrate on being kids.

While I'm not advocating continual interference in day-to-day issues or parents who storm the principal's office in righteous indignation, I am suggesting that you take a stand against the bigger issues: namely: injustice, inhumanity and policies that jeopardize the safety of the children at your school.

To give you an example, allow me to share an incident that happened in my son's kindergarten class. On this particular day, I was acting as a chaperone for a field trip. Before we left, the teacher announced that she had a surprise for the kids. One of the eggs in the incubator had hatched.

As each group of children came up to the incubator, there were delighted giggles, squeals and excited "oohs" and "aahs." After the last group of children had seen the chick, we filed outside and boarded the bus. When we returned, I was the first mom off the bus and instructed the children to line up against the wall in front of the door to the kindergarten classroom. One student asked my permission to go inside, but I told him that he would have to wait until his teacher was in the room. As it turned out, this was a good decision because when the kindergarten teacher entered the room from inside the school, she discovered that the newborn chick had been taken from the incubator and stomped to death. The downy hatchling that had delighted the kids two short hours earlier had been reduced to a mangled, bloody clump of guts.

Horrified by the news, the chaperones kept the children outside on the playground and retrieved their backpacks from the classroom. Later, I was told that an older student who comes to the kindergarten playground at recess to supervise had admitted to committing this heinous act. There were bloody footprints leading away from the scene and the child was found in his classroom with blood smeared across the bottom of his shoes. The school authorities assured the parents that this boy would be expelled from school.

Although many parents were satisfied that the authorities had acted swiftly and justly, I felt that something terrible had gone awry, so I began asking questions. Later that day, I talked to my eldest son (then, a third grader) and learned that the kindergarten children share the same recess time as the third and fourth graders. Although they have recess at the same time, they play in separate areas.

After asking my eldest son more questions, I found out that the third and fourth graders who are sent to supervise the kindergarten children are the "kids who are always in trouble." Apparently, the school authorities punish these kids by making them watch "the babies" and give up recess with their peers.

I asked my eldest son about the third grade "supervisors." He told me that they were the bullies, the kids who were always picking on their smaller and weaker peers.

Later, I found out the name of the kid who had killed the chick in the kindergarten class. He happened to be a student in my eldest son's class. This kid was a known bully. In fact, one week prior to this incident, during our daily discussion after school, my son had announced as he pressed his index finger and thumb together, that his teacher had said that the boy was "this close to being suspended."

As these facts clicked in my brain, I realized that although it might have appeared to some parents that the school had taken appropriate action, it was the school that had made it possible for the third grader to commit this act in the first place. When the next week came, my son told me that the boy still had not been expelled.

Feeling as though I had enough information, I called the school secretary and made an appointment to meet with the principal and the guidance counselor, the two individuals who had designed the bully reform program.

Our initial meeting was scheduled and rescheduled three times. Wondering if they were avoiding me, I went to the office unannounced and said that I wanted to see the principal.

After taking a seat, I told the principal that I was disturbed by the incident that had happened in the kindergarten class and wanted to know why the older child (whom we'll call David) was supervising the kindergarten children.

She replied that it was none of my business.

Undeterred, I pointed out to the principal that she and the guidance counselor had set up David and the kindergarten class. Although she vehemently denied it, I continued to explain why this was so, until I saw that she was beginning to understand. By placing a known bully in the charge of younger, more vulnerable kids, she had given him easy targets for his aggression. Although it was tragic that a baby chick had been killed, she was lucky that David hadn't hurt one of the kindergarten children.

The principal's assumption that taking care of younger children would create compassion in the bully was naïve and denied all we know about bully psychology. As a parent, it seems reasonable to believe that school authorities with many years of experience understand how bullies prey on younger, weaker kids.

As a parent, you can't afford to make assumptions such as this. I told the principal that by placing a known bully in the care of kindergarten children, she had jeopardized their safety. I also told her that this third grade bully had showed her through his actions exactly what he thought of her reform program. I told her that until she acknowledged this, I didn't feel safe enough to leave my children at her school.

When the principal conceded my point, I felt the kids were safe again. While parents can't expect school authorities to know everything, it's reassuring when they admit their errors and illustrate a willingness to grow. Although this principal later left our school, I felt confident that we had learned something of value from each other.

As guardians, we have a responsibility to keep watch over each other and offer insight when adults in charge seem to miss the bigger picture. In this way, we become guardians of the guardians and join together in our shared responsibility for the children of the world.

The Circles of Love and Influence

Native American philosophy is based on the circle because it reveals life's content and the context in which it unfolds. The parent-child relationship consists of circles that are created through love and bonding. These circles ripple out and touch everyone with whom your child comes in contact.

The first circle is the bond between male and female that is consummated in the act of making love. The sperm unites with the egg to create a fertilized egg—the single cell that contains everything it needs to grow into a human being. The cell divides, differentiates and develops into a fetus. The fetus is suspended in a sphere-like womb and attended by the placenta, which delivers nourishment and removes waste via a circuit-like pathway. Next comes the birth of the child (or what I refer to as the "birth of mutuality"), during which female gives birth to child and child gives birth to mother. As the new-born baby suckles at the mother's breast, each encircles the other and the bonds of humanity are formed.

The rules of the circle are few and simple and form the basis for future bonds. The circle contains all it needs for its completion. The circle is all-inclusive. In the circle, everyone is equal. Circles expand and self-replicate. What is given to the circle is returned.

As you raise your child, keep the tenets of the circle in mind and reflect upon its deeper meaning. Your relationship with your child creates a circle of influence that expands as your child goes out into the world and has relationships with others. Like Kevote in *Spirit-Boy and the Gift of Turquoise,* the good medicine you give your child will become part of his offering to others. In this way, the parent-child relationship transcends itself in an ever-widening arc that extends to family, friends and community at-large.

Embracing Parenthood

As adults, we are unprepared for parenthood because until we've raised children of our own, we have no real concept of what it means to be a caretaker. Adults who have an idealized notion of parenting will have difficulty meeting its demands.

Parenting is messy, but all human bonding occurs through the exchange of messy emotions and bodily fluids. There will be mother's milk, blood, sweat, vomit, urine, snot, threats, accusations, belly laughs, I-love-you's, I-hate-you's, excrement and lots of tears. When you first become a mother, your body will seem as though it no longer belongs to you, as it responds instinctually to your child.

I'll never forget what happened after I had my second child, Colt. I gave birth to him in the middle of the college semester, while I was working on my masters. After his birth, I took a week off and returned to class when he was eight days old. I hired a babysitter, who accompanied me to the university, so she could watch my son in an adjacent room, while I attended a creative writing class. I arrived early, nursed my child in the empty room and rocked him to sleep, hoping he would sleep through the two hour class. Knowing that he might awaken, I gave the babysitter a bottle filled with milk.

During class, I was called upon to read aloud a story I had written. About two minutes into reading it, my son began to cry. Although his cries were muffled by the wall between us, my body responded instantly. As I struggled to keep my focus on the words, breast milk soaked through my pads and dripped down the front of my shirt. There was nothing I could do to stop or cover it up and after a few tense moments, I realized that responding to my child was the choice to make. I told the teacher that I'd have to read my story later. It could wait, but my child could not. I went into the room with the near-frantic babysitter who was trying her best to quiet my screaming newborn who was smart enough to refuse both a substitute mother and a phony nipple.

As I comforted my child, one of the students poked her head into the room and invited me to bring the baby into class. I took him into the other room, where he nursed happily. The smiles I received from other students were supportive and encouraging. Although none of them were parents, they recognized the immediacy of the baby's hunger and knew that in the scheme of things, he came first.

The bonding (and seeming bondage) of the baby years will prepare you for the years to come. The bloody birth and fluid exchange that come from having and caring for an infant form the adhesive that bonds parent to child and child to parent. During the baby years, you might trick yourself into believing that these are the challenging times and the easy part is yet to come. Instead as your child grows, you'll find that rather than lessening, your responsibilities deepen in a way that requires greater balance, vision and maturity on your part. As your child grows, you are challenged to grow as well.

In many ways, your current family resembles your family-of-origin. Although you chose your mate, you didn't choose your children, nor did they choose you. Children have a variety of temperaments, some more challenging than others. Like anyone who is close to you, they will learn to push your buttons, but if you begin to see that by doing so, they unwittingly present you with the lessons you need to learn, you will embrace parenthood as an opportunity for growth.

During the most trying times, you might complain that you didn't sign up for this. Your children will break your favorite things, color on the walls, drain your pocketbook, repeat what you've said in private in public, keep you up all night and invade rare moments of solitude. Delightfully demanding little creatures that they are, they will take all you have to give and steal your heart as well. As they hold it in their pudgy, little Buddha hands, they'll challenge you to blossom like a flower that unfolds its shimmering petals in the light.

As you fully realize your role as guardian, you will become a facilitator of the I-Thou dialogue, a dispenser of good medicine and the keeper of your child's heart, mind, body, spirit, worldview and self-perceptions. Although at times it will seem as though life makes this more challenging than it must, the more you embrace your role as caretaker, the more you will discover the wisdom of the heart. During such experiences, the true reciprocity between the keeper and the kept will be revealed and you will know that parenting is not a duty, but a privilege and an opportunity. Again and again you will realize this as the spark of love that initiates every heartfelt action reveals a radiance that transcends the relationship that gave it birth.

Chapter 3

The Nature of Identity

*A child who is raised to know his nature
grows up to lead a purposeful life.*

Encouraging Your Child's Quest for Identity

The quest for human identity is the journey of a lifetime. Some people lead their lives without ever truly knowing themselves, while others take an entire lifetime to catch a glimmer of who they are. Those who fail to know their nature lead a life of self-confusion, self-destruction, rage and desperation. Although they have never known their nature, they feel the tragedy of its loss.

Like an adult, a child's emotional and spiritual needs are met by discovering who he is and how he can contribute to his family and the world. A child who knows himself and heeds his inner voice will grow up to find his purpose. Purposeful living creates meaning and fulfillment.

Knowing yourself and finding your purpose give you a place in life. Like a star in the evening sky, you're connected to other stars and everything in the cosmos. You shed your light into the darkness, allowing others to see and revealing a frequency that is uniquely yours. In giving what you are here to give, you feel a sense of place, meaning and connection to something bigger than yourself.

Giving your child the tools to lead a fulfilling life is the greatest expression of parental love. Are you willing to teach your child to lead a purposeful life, even if you aren't yet doing so yourself?

Think about the alternative. Look around and you will see it—the dull despair or silent rage behind some people's eyes. But you don't need to look any further than their actions. You can see it in people who self-medicate with alcohol or drugs. You can see it in those who have traded their passion for a job that pays, but slowly robs them of their soul.

The philosopher, Joseph Campbell, once said, "The privilege of a lifetime is knowing who you are." This privilege is earned by finding the courage to express what is in your heart. It is the inner world that gives birth to our experience of the outer.

As a parent, one of the most generous gifts you can give your child is to show him how to earn this privilege. You can do it even if you haven't earned it yet yourself. In teaching your child to know his heart, you'll come face to face with your nature.

Let's take Joseph Campbell's quote and apply it to parenthood: *The privilege of parenting is getting to know your child.* By helping your child discover who he is, you'll experience the depths of parent-child intimacy and uncover yourself more fully in the process. For those who haven't yet walked the path of self-discovery, parenthood offers a second chance.

Embracing Humbleness

My husband, Larry Ramirez, is a Native American psychotherapist. In his tribe, it is believed that man is the humblest of all creatures because he is born without direction. In order to find his way in life, man must find his nature. This is the purpose behind the Vision Quest.

Unlike humans, animals are born "knowing" who they are. Although an animal may not consciously *know* himself, he follows his instincts which make him behave like the animal he is.

In Chapter 2, I shared a children's story I wrote called *How Coyote and Beaver Became Good Friends.* As you may remember, Beaver takes ill and Coyote invites him to his den to nurse him back to health. Coyote kills several small animals for his friend to eat, but Beaver isn't interested. Without proper nourishment, Beaver grows weaker until finally he refuses water. Frightened that his friend will die, Coyote paces outside by the pond. When he notices the differences between his den and Beaver's dam, he realizes how different coyotes and beavers are. Knowing this helps Coyote see beyond himself and recognize the nature of another being.

Like animals, we have physical needs, but we also have emotional, mental and spiritual needs. We recognize animals by observing what they *do*; we know ourselves by *doing* what we *love*.

Animals instinctually "know" themselves, while humans have to "find" themselves. While this distinction should make us humble and encourage us to become students of the natural world, it makes us arrogant instead. It's an arrogance borne of fear because behind our claim that the brain and its technology can solve life's mysteries, are a bunch of humans who deny their basic nature.

Man's fear of nature has divorced him from the animal world. In his arrogance, he assumes that his claim to consciousness elevates him above it, but consciousness without conscientiousness makes us less than human. Rather than embracing the mystery and allowing it to unfold, man seeks to control, dissect and destroy it. He hasn't realized that the Nature that surrounds him is a metaphor of self that leads to an understanding of *his* nature and a profound grasp of the universe.

To find your nature, you must accept that unlike animals, you were born without direction. Although it may seem scary at first, accept it. Rather than hiding behind your intellect, let helping your child discover his nature become part of your Vision Quest and a developmental task for you both. As a human being, this is one of the greatest adventures you will ever undertake. As a parent, it is a privilege to witness your child's spiritual unfolding.

Although this book will not specifically teach you how to find *your* nature, as you assist in your child's *becoming*, you'll touch your essence many times.

Creation Unfolding

Nature is our greatest teacher and shows herself in a myriad of forms. When we align ourselves with Nature, we glean her secrets. Like any clever teacher, Nature's language is couched in symbolism that leads toward subjective truth. Through observance of the natural world, we discover our nature, the order of things and the possibility of transcendence.

In *The Biology of Transcendence*, Joseph Chilton Pearce points out that Nature repeats the history of our evolution each time a human fetus is conceived. At conception, each of us begins life as a single cell that replicates into many. As cell differentiation takes place, the fetus develops gills, a tail and slowly achieves a more human-looking form.

In this way, Nature shows us that we have all emerged from the same primordial soup.

Pearce emphasizes that the structure of the human brain also reveals our evolution. We are born with a triune brain—a reptilian brain, enfolded by a mammalian brain, topped by the uniquely human prefrontal cortex.

At birth, a baby has one hundred billion neurons. These neurons emerged from a single cell that began its evolution in the womb. Stimulation from the child's environment causes the neurons to migrate throughout the brain, specialize and connect the various structures. The environment is the stimulus for reinforcing certain pathways and pruning others. As Pearce points out, the brain mirrors its early environment while building a structure that can survive it. Love and bonding create interconnections that increase complexity, function and the capacity to thrive.

The prefrontal cortex gives us the capability to reason, to create art and written language—something other mammals cannot do. But there is a price for this higher function—a heightened sense of responsibility. Since Native Americans believed that form follows function, they knew that our *capacity* for higher awareness is what dictates our *responsibility* as caretakers of the Earth.

What mainstream American culture has seen historically as its relationship to Earth is not a relationship at all because its focus has been on man's *power over* Earth, rather than his *place* in it. Our relationship with Earth reflects our ability to relate to others, particularly our children. The basic difference in philosophies between mainstream and native cultures explains why white people once viewed their children as possessions, while Native Americans saw children as spiritual equals.

The white man's tendency to separate the part from the whole in an attempt to comprehend it means that he often misses a bigger truth. To truly understand the nature of a thing, we must observe it within its context. For example, if you spot a spider crawling across your picnic table, you may swat it because you see it as a pest. However, when you view the spider within the context of its environment, you realize that its function is to help control the insect population and protect the delicate balance of life on Earth.

Our tendency to focus on the content, while ignoring the context is a habit that divides us along political, cultural and religious lines. A good example of this is the conflict between the evolutionists and the creationists. Whenever people have a piece of the puzzle, they divide into separate camps and cling rigidly to their view. As David Hawkins points out in *The Eye of the I*, in defending their positions, such people miss a higher truth: evolution *is* the unfolding of creation. Creation *contains* the seeds of evolution. Each gives rise to the other in a stunningly dynamic interplay. In much the same way, your child assists in your *becoming* as you strive to teach and model for him what it means to be a mature human being.

When you understand this, you see what Native Americans have long known—human beings are life's keepers. Although we have evolved past life's lower forms, they are not *below* us, but *within* us. We are connected to everything because we have passed through all life's permutations.

To substantiate this, recent research by the Heart Math Institute has discovered neurons in the heart. This makes the heart our fourth brain. Like the triune structure in our head, the heart evolves through appreciation, love and caring. The heart determines who we are, what we love and what we have to give.

Animals *know* themselves by following their instincts, while humans *find* themselves by following the heart. The heart is the *organ of purpose and direction*. The heart determines nature. Native Americans have long known what science is only beginning to divine. As Jimalee Burton of the Ho-Chee-Nee tribe once said, "The white man thinks with his head—the Indian thinks with his heart."

Development of the parental heart is fostered through love and caring. In this way, your relationship with your child provides you with many chances to unfold the petals of your heart. Instead of relying solely on the brain's ability to separate, learn to use the integrative function of the heart.

Development of the child's heart is facilitated through his relationship with others and a growing awareness of who he is and what he loves.

Although brain development and physical growth is believed to stop in the late teens or early twenties, development of the heart—the fourth brain and vehicle of transcendence—is ongoing and culminates in the adult realization of purpose, compassion and oneness. The evolution of your heart begins with the physical, emotional, mental and spiritual stewardship of your child. Borrowing Native American terminology, we may refer to these as the Four Directions of parenting.

Nature is our teacher and our Heaven here on Earth. Heaven is waiting to be discovered in each minute expression of God's nature—in you, in me and particularly, in our children who are fresh from the lap of God.

The Truth about Cats and Dogs

Most people don't realize that Native Americans were the first psychologists because they understood that observation of the animal world gave them a basic understanding of human nature. Rather than holing yourself up in the forest to learn nature's secrets, start in your own backyard. Begin with what you know about cats and dogs.

Although cats and dogs are both animals, they have different natures. For the most part, cats are independent, while dogs are more reliant upon relationship. If you approach a cat, she might snub you, but most dogs won't turn down your affection. You might roughhouse your dog to show your love, but you would never rough up a cat.

Although there are generalities that apply to certain classes of animals, there are unique differences within each type. For instance, my akita, Cochise, turns his nose up at bread, while my akita, Basheen, performs tricks for it. Believe it or not, this dog chooses bread over meat. Knowing my dogs' likes and dislikes enables me to honor their differences and acknowledge their uniqueness.

It's the same with children. Paying attention to what they like or dislike is how you begin to see their nature.

Different animals must be treated differently because their nature requires it. Things are no different in the human world. You can't raise two children in exactly the same manner because the differences in their nature create a dynamic, which determines how *you* act. If you fool yourself into thinking that treating your kids exactly the same is fair, then you're committing an injustice. First of all, it can't be done. Second and more importantly, by failing to recognize the differences between your children, you deny the uniqueness of their nature.

In America, many of us celebrate the differences between ethnic groups, while a few do not. The same thing happens in families. Some parents celebrate their children's differences, while others pretend that all children are the same. In addition to being lazy, this is inhumane. It is the parents who are afraid of life and don't know themselves who force their children to become replicas of each other or of themselves. Such parents are often envious of their children's high energy, passionate curiosity and firm knowledge of their preferences because it reminds them that they've barely scratched the surface of their lives.

A child lives deeply and fully. A child is in the moment. For a mother who was seldom permitted to experience this freedom as a child, it might be difficult to witness her child enjoying what she was forbidden. It's not that such parents don't want a better life for their children, but that the child's expression of freedom acts as a trigger for their unconscious rage at never having had the opportunity to experience this themselves.

Although your child may look like you, he is not you. He may mimic your behavior, he may swallow your beliefs, but he is *not* you. One of the most tragic errors that you can make as a parent is to shape your child into what I call a "mini-me." Don't make the mistake that Kevote made in *Spirit-Boy and the Gift of Turquoise*. It's an error that sacrifices your relationship and symbolically or literally, can cost your child his life.

When thinking about the importance of knowing your child's nature, consider this: it is the nature of a bird to fly. While no one questions the unfolding of a bird's abilities, parents often deny their children's natural gifts. By doing so, they clip their wings before they've had the chance to try them. A child who has never had the opportunity to test his wings has little hope of reaching his true potential. This is a tragic loss for all of us. Parents who are compelled to make their child into a mini-me do so because on some level, they yearn to relive their childhood. These parents had parents who fashioned them into their likeness. And so the torch is passed.

A Family of Many Species

The natural world is comprised of many different animals. Each class of animals has a nature and there are individual differences within each type. Your family is no different.

Although you share the same genetics, your family can be viewed as a pack of dissimilar "animals" because each person has a different nature. As a parent, your job is to see and *encourage* your child's recognition of her nature. Turning to Mother Nature will illustrate this point.

In the jungle, there are gorillas, elephants and piranhas. Even if you've never been to the jungle, you know you wouldn't see a gorilla acting like a fish. This doesn't happen in the animal kingdom, but in the human world, it happens all the time.

In the human jungle, human "monkeys" act like human "tigers" because they don't know what animal they are. Perhaps because we've grown up with the knowledge that we're all human, we assume this means we're all the same. But there are many different "animals" in the human world. The first step in knowing ourselves is to recognize our nature.

This fact of nature is seldom acknowledged in schools where children's behavior is normalized and individual expressions are often discouraged. It's not recognized in families in which parents lump their children into the same category in an effort to make things easy or fair. Of course, doing so is neither fair nor just. And it's certainly not easy on the child. A parent's failure to recognize and encourage her child's nature is at the root of human desperation.

If your child doesn't know his nature, he doesn't have a basic understanding of himself. Such a child grows up alienated from his heart. He feels like a fraud when he notices that his behavior is not consistent and that his 'values' are predicated upon the situation or whom he's with. He develops a tendency toward self-righteousness and becomes a public and/or private critic of others. As harsh as he is with others, he's even harsher with himself. As he grows, he tries to push away the void of self-despair with alcohol, drugs, sex, overwork or other forms of excessiveness. The faster he runs from the void, the more it consumes him because it is within.

Getting to know your child's nature is a privilege. In no other endeavor in life, do you have the opportunity to nurture the growth of something as beautiful or profound.

Remember that those who consider themselves above the animal world are lost because they have misplaced the thread that connects them to the natural world and to their nature. Although this is probably the opposite of what you've been taught, please consider the value of these words. The animal kingdom is symbolic of the human world and there is much that it can teach us.

The first and most important lesson that we can learn from our animal brothers and sisters is that unlike them, we were born without direction. In order to find our purpose in life, each individual must find his or her own way.

The Nature of Nature

If you have more than one child, then you know that each of your children was born with a unique personality. Although experience shapes a child, she is more than a product of her environment. Even though your child's genetics determine her appearance and aspects of her personality, she is more than her genetic profile. Although your love nurtures and encourages her, she is more than a product of your love.

Your child's nature is the essence that grounds her in the physical world. Although love and experience will set her along a certain course, her nature reveals her purpose here on Earth.

A child's nature is intangible and is known through its expression. Like the natural world around us, it's a mystery of sorts. Although lack of love and repeated trauma can disconnect a child from his nature, at its core, it is unalterable.

Your child's nature can be likened to the wind: although you can hear it rustling through the leaves and watch it quiver through tall grasses, it is invisible, except through its effects. Nature is revealed through its continuum—the wind can be creative or destructive—it can seed the land with wildflowers, cool and sweep the planet or it can rip apart your home. A child's nature is much the same, except that its expressions can be channeled by parental love. When tempered with humanity, it expresses itself positively. If ignored or broken through cruelty or harsh indoctrination, it destroys itself and others.

Teaching your child about her nature helps her to own her inner strengths. Teaching her that her uniqueness is a gift to give the world will inspire her to develop it and make a contribution that benefits us all. As your child's strengths grow, she will begin to recognize the special qualities in others and encourage them to shine. This is crucial in today's world in which so many people believe that happiness exists outside them.

Raising your child to know her nature encourages self-direction. Self-direction is the compass that will guide your child through the perils of adolescence and around the traps of indoctrination. For some it is experienced as a voice, a thrum, or an inner stillness; for others it is a vision, an impulse or a knowing. However it is experienced, it is a call to take the leap of faith that initiates the journey of unfolding.

Help your child find this path by teaching her about the natural world. Discuss the nature of different plants and animals. Teach her to know animals by what they *do*: dogs bark, cats meow and birds chirp.

Once she understands the natural world, teach her that in the human world, things are not always what they seem. Human animals often reveal themselves in covert ways: what they say doesn't always coincide with what they do, particularly in times of opportunity or conflict. Since your child will have already been primed by her observations of the natural world, she'll have an easier time spotting the different animals that comprise the human race.

Losing and Finding the Way

When babies are born into the world, they are connected to their center. They cry when they are hungry and smile when they feel happy. Their ability to communicate their feelings through facial and vocal expressions gives parents the cues to meet their needs.

As children emerge from the toddler years, they learn that certain expressions are unacceptable in certain situations. Expressions that were previously met with open arms may be met now with disapproval, as parents attempt to "grow up baby" and socialize their child. This can be a confusing time for children because they're used to being encouraged. While yesterday, they were applauded for their ability to talk, walk and run, now their parents tell them to sit still and be quiet. Although children must learn to live with others, it's tragic that they often lose themselves in the process. During the socialization process, all children are at risk for this. When children are taught to deny their feelings and sacrifice themselves for others, they suffer what I call a "rupture of the heart."

The road back to the heart is not straight and narrow, but circuitous. In this way, losing the self may be part of finding it. Although a rupture of the heart may be an unavoidable consequence of human socialization, there are certain precautions that can be taken to lessen its severity, so that a child grows up with a strong, intact sense of self.

When utilized by parents, these precautions become proactive strategies that help children stay attuned to their nature, even as they are learning how to live harmoniously with others. These strategies include: polishing the stone, naming nature, engaging interests and helping your child become people-smart. Using these strategies will help your child know herself, claim her strengths and follow the compass of the heart.

Polishing the Turquoise

In my husband's tribe, when a woman is pregnant, it is said that she has a piece of turquoise inside her womb. When that turquoise is born into the world, it is the parents' job to polish it until its matrix is revealed.

Each piece of turquoise has a different matrix. The matrix is a symbol of a child's uniqueness. Since turquoise is a mix of green and blue—of Earth and Sky—it represents the union of form and spirit. Your child came through you, but he is *not* you because his matrix is different from yours.

This striking metaphor aptly describes our role as parents. Our job is to help our children find their uniqueness, so they can give it to the world. Helping your child find himself is an honor. Not only have you had the privilege of being present at his physical birth, you have the opportunity to witness the unfolding of his spiritual nature.

Like Kevote in *Spirit-Boy and the Gift of Turquoise,* your job is to encourage what your child loves. By *polishing the turquoise* with love and wonder, you reveal its matrix—the gift the Creator placed in each child's heart. The expression of this gift gives a child a sense of purpose. Purpose leads to contribution, self-actualization and personal fulfillment.

The matrix in the turquoise is a unique expression of nature that has never existed before and will never exist again. Without it, life is meaningless. This is why the greatest quest we undertake in life is the search for identity. It's a universal quest that cuts across both time and culture. As a generation that has been influenced by New Age beliefs, we must embrace the knowledge that we only have *this* lifetime in which to claim our strengths and make a difference. Even if you believe in multiple lives, you must not allow this to guide you because then it becomes too easy to be lazy or give up entirely if you think that your work can be continued in another life.

You have this life to make an impact. Never again will you exist in this way, in this body, with these particular characteristics, in this family comprised of these personality types and in this specific space-time continuum. Your nature combined with the insights gleaned from personal experience enables you to realize your purpose here on Earth.

The most spiritual task of parenthood requires helping your child find his nature and giving him the tools to reconnect with it during trying times. If you're still searching for your nature, then you can appreciate the gift a parent gives when she acts as a mentor from the start, helping to ground her child in the realization of his nature.

Although I've quoted Thoreau before, his words are appropriate here again: "Most men lead lives of quiet desperation." To this I reply that a child who is taught to follow his nature will create a fulfilling life. If you help your child uncover his interests and abilities at each stage of development, he will grow up expressing his natural gifts. In this way, he will not have to lose himself to find himself because he will have been living from his center all along.

Naming Nature

For centuries, parents have provided for their children's physical needs and thought that was enough. In Maslow's "Hierarchy of Human Needs" the physical is first. While taking care of physical and emotional needs may have been sufficient one hundred years ago, now that modern conveniences have afforded us leisure time and time for self-reflection, we've become increasingly aware of our spiritual needs. In a society that is disconnected from Nature, it is crucial to be connected to the self. As parents who envision the highest for our children, we must help them find their nature (or "spiritual intelligence"), so they move beyond a life of mere survival and learn what it means to thrive.

This is accomplished in other cultures through naming ceremonies. In the Native American culture, typically, the grandmother gives the child his spiritual name. Among native peoples, you're not a real woman, until you've become a *grand*mother because by then, you have polished the turquoise heart of many a child. The same is true of a grandfather—you become a real man after you've done what is necessary to raise a child into an adult who is *mature* enough to raise children of his own. Once again, we see the emphasis on stewardship and how action determines role—in this case, naming the nature of a child.

Giving a child a spiritual name serves four purposes. First, it distinguishes him from other members of the family or tribe. A child who knows his nature has a strong sense of identity. His name is proof that his uniqueness has been acknowledged by the elders of the tribe.

Second, his spiritual name gives him a sense of belonging to something greater than himself. A spiritual name is something that he grows into. This gives him a sense of responsibility to himself and others because he has a name that he must live up to and a purpose to unfold.

Third, a spiritual name gives him a sense of meaning and direction. Within his nature are the seeds of his awakening—his identity, means of belonging and contribution to the whole.

Fourth, his spiritual name is a form of self-preservation that grounds him securely to the Earth. While a child's given name may be Frank, his spiritual name may be "Running Deer." (Keep in mind that Native American spiritual names are given in native languages, rather than in English.) The fact that this image has an action attached to it reminds him that in order to be realized his nature must be expressed. Since the vehicle of expression is the body, the child learns that he must care for it in order to allow its full articulation. In this way, the physical and the spiritual are intertwined. The image conjured by his spiritual name which is a metaphor-in-motion connects him with the apparent and subtle attributes of his nature from which he will take direction, despite external circumstances. For instance, when Frank is feeling down, the powerful attributes of his spiritual name will call him from his isolation and remind him of his purpose. In this way, his spiritual name gives him a sense of inner power that helps him rise above the struggles and trivialities of life.

Although naming rituals originated with Native Americans and other indigenous cultures, don't worry that such a practice will conflict with your religious beliefs. Religion is defined as a particular faith and its means of worship, while spirituality focuses on our connections to self and others. In this sense, religion is the content, while spirituality is the context. Where religion divides us into separate camps, spirituality unites us in our humanness. The techniques described herein are spiritual and will not conflict with your beliefs.

Before we can connect to others, we must have a means of feeling connected to the self. There's no better illustration of spirituality than in the interconnectedness of Nature. This is why finding our nature and naming it is not a religious practice, but a spiritual task because in nature, we find our gift to others.

We need people. We need each others' strengths. Each child needs to find out who he is, so he can weave his own glistening strand into the web.

Giving Your Child a Spiritual Name

To choose your child's spiritual name, look at his strengths, attributes and what he loves to do. Watch your child for a couple of days and notice what he most enjoys doing with his body. Does he like to jump, whistle, tumble, sing, whisper, screech, dance, smile, run, laugh or giggle? Notice an activity in which he engages with abandon and write it down.

Make a list of your child's attributes. Is he strong, smart, fast, quick, caring, courageous, adventurous, happy-go-lucky, kind-hearted, loving, curious, industrious, affectionate, patient, creative, contemplative, fierce or loyal? Record his strengths. Take a week or so and read these attributes during quiet moments. You might not get an animal image right away, but sooner or later, it will come—maybe while you're vacuuming or in the shower, while you're driving, falling asleep at night or awakening in the morning. When the image comes, write it down.

Combine the action with the animal name. For instance, you might have a name like, "Spinning Tiger," "Dancing Mouse" or

"Laughing Hawk." Don't worry if the action seems to contradict the nature of the animal. Trust what comes. Don't shy away from names like "squirrel" or "monkey" due to unflattering connotations, although for the benefit of your child, I recommend that you choose animals that are native to your continent. What is most important is that the name aptly captures your child's strengths and what he likes to do.

Don't worry that you may not have picked the *right* spiritual name. There is not *one* right name. As your child matures, the deeper meaning of his spiritual name will be revealed to him through his interests, experiences, insights and reflections. It's not up to you to assign a meaning to his name—your challenge is to choose a name that most accurately depicts his physicality and attributes as a child. What is most important is that this name connects him to a place and time when he was most connected to and expressive of his nature. If a child is in that preconscious stage, when he's not yet been indoctrinated with what he's *supposed to be* or how he's *supposed to act*, he instinctively follows his nature, although he's unaware of it. Through his physical proclivities and natural strengths, he's closer to his animal spirit than perhaps at any other time.

While it is up to you to carefully choose your child's spiritual name, it is up to him to discover its meaning. Meaning is personal and has many levels of interpretation, so as long as you commit yourself to seeing what is before you, you will come up with a resourceful name.

Positively associate your child with his spiritual name. For instance, if you have a child who likes to climb and leap off things and you see him engaging in these activities, say with enthusiasm, "There's my Climbing Cougar." If your child is fiercely loyal and protective, when she displays these attributes say, "You are like the wolf: fierce, yet protective of your loved ones." If your child is wild and free, she could remind you of animals as different as a hawk or mustang. The label matters less than the feeling of authenticity it evokes.

If your child is at least five years old, you can create a ceremony in which you give him his spiritual name. This can be as simple as creating a quiet space, lighting a candle and telling him that now that he's older and you have seen what is in his heart, you are giving him a spiritual name that describes his nature. Explain that this is different from his given name because it is private and will only be used in a sacred way by those who truly know him. It is a name that celebrates the best in him and the things he likes to do. It's a tool to help him remember how strong he is when he forgets. (Older children can be given animal spirit necklaces that are emblematic of their nature. See the Resources page at the end of this book. For a description of the naming ceremony that I gave my children, see the parenting workbook that is available from my web site.)

The author, Hermann Hesse once said, "Every man has only one genuine vocation: to find the way to himself." Since it's a hobby of mine to take great quotes and alter them in a manner that best serves parenting, I'll take the liberty of misquoting Mr. Hesse: *"Every parent has one genuine duty: to help their child find the way to himself."* As a parent, make this your number one rule of engagement.

Engaging Your Child's Interests

In American society, 'quiet desperation' runs deep. We have more money, education and leisure time than any other nation in the world, yet from a big perspective, these surface achievements haven't improved the quality of our lives or deepened our relationships with our children. In fact, the source of quiet desperation can often be traced back to childhood—to cruel or indifferent parents or parents who spent little time or had no interest in their kids.

Although this sounds discouraging, there is a cure. The medicine for 'quiet desperation' is a daily dose of passion. Your child's passionate interests reveal his nature and unveil his purpose. This means that parents must encourage their children's interests.

Keeping children attuned to their interests is fairly easy because they're extremely vocal regarding the subjects about which they care. The key is to learn how to *listen.* Many parents hear, but do not listen. According to *The New Oxford American Dictionary, listen* comes from the Old English *hlynan,* which means to "pay attention." While hearing engages your ears in the perception of sounds, listening engages the heart and mind in true communication. The art of listening requires you to be alert to the cues beyond the words. Paying attention in this way helps you to perceive what your child is trying to communicate, which is not always the same as what he says.

You've heard the old saying: "Children should be seen and not heard." Although this was a common saying thirty years ago, it's not used much today. If you discard one saying in your parents' or grandparents' bag of quips, make it this one. Children must be seen and heard and in order to feel loved and cherished, they must be *listened to.*

When you listen to your child, you acknowledge him. When this happens with consistency, a child feels *seen* in his entirety, which fosters bonding and a feeling of self-worth. When a child gets your attention by sharing stories, concerns or interests, he won't need to get your attention in negative ways. In fact, ploys for negative attention may be signs that your child is crying to be listened to.

Listening to your child is your way of being present—of being there for him. Remember that listening requires much more than hearing words. It's an embrace of the whole person: his demeanor, facial expressions, posture, body language, tone, content, subtext and understanding of his nature. When you listen, you establish a connection. Without this, your child will fall into trouble and despair.

When your child shares her passions with you, consider it a gift. If you're financially minded, think of it as an investment. Your child is the investor and you are the bank. When your child invests you with her passion, give it back *with interest.* You do this by listening attentively, asking questions and physically engaging your child. This may require playing a game of catch, making a finger-painting or watching your child's favorite show. When you ask your child a question about her interests, she'll feel a surge of pride at being able to answer it, particularly when she knows that you didn't know the answer. This will allow her to feel like she knows something, which will inspire her to engage her interests further. There's no greater rush for a child than to feel that she can help someone or teach someone something that she knows. Since sharing interests requires the art of conversation, it's magical in the sense that it connects two hearts in space and time.

When you learn to "listen with your blood," as one of my teachers used to say, you engage your child in full contact with your love. In its highest terms, loving another means having a genuine interest in their highest good, which requires encouraging them to know their nature and follow their dreams. Any other form of parental "love" is rooted in self-interest, which is driven by dependency or the desire for control.

Poke-MOM

Although the Pokemon® craze may have passed somewhat, it provides an excellent model for how you can engage your child's interests to communicate abstract concepts and teach him about nature. In case you're not familiar with this phenomenon, Pokemon are cartoon characters who duel each other. The main character is a young boy named, Ash, who teaches Pokemon how to use their strengths to evolve to higher levels. Since Ash aspires to be the best Pokemon trainer in the world, he is evolving too.

There are many things I like about Pokemon. The first is that although there is some violence because the characters duel, when a character loses, he faints, rather than dying.

Second, Pokemon are identified by various elements of nature. There are Leaf Pokemon, Fire Pokemon, Water Pokemon, etc. The strengths and weaknesses of the Pokemon derive from their classification and follow Mother Nature's rules. For instance a Fire Pokemon can beat a Leaf Pokemon because fire can burn a leaf.

Third, when a Pokemon uses his strengths to battle another Pokemon and wins, he evolves to a higher level. As a mother, who encourages her children to know their strengths and how to channel them, Pokemon provides a means of teaching the principles of human growth at their level of comprehension. As such, I've dubbed myself "Poke-Mom" and tell my children that I'm their Poke-trainer and that it is my job to help them use their strengths to gain a better understanding of their nature.

Fourth, although Pokemon characters evolve by learning how best to use their strengths in a variety of situations, there are unscrupulous Poketrainers, who force their Pokemon to evolve prematurely. Although the creature appears to be evolved, it lacks the benefit of training, so it usually loses to lower level Pokemon.

As you can see, there's some great material in Pokemon for teaching children how to recognize their nature, use their strengths when faced with challenges and take the steps necessary for lasting growth. Since the Pokemon characters are evolving, children learn that they are evolving too.

In this way, I've used my children's passionate interests to create a language by which I can teach them abstract concepts. While some parents are sick and tired of hearing about Pokemon, I've used my boys' interests to mutual benefit.

This is one way that parents can connect with children. If you learn to speak a language that has captured your child's imagination, then you can communicate with him on a level that transcends words and speaks directly to his heart. When you understand this concept, your relationship evolves to a higher level.

In order to communicate in this way, start by embracing one of your child's interests. Once you understand its symbolism and basic premise, you can create a bridge of communication. The best way to learn about your child's interests is to allow him to teach you. In addition to making an opportunity for him to spend time with you, it creates a sense of intimacy and allows you to see into his heart.

When you learn to speak the language of your child's heart, you can convey values and complex constructs in such a way that he will embrace them as his own. In this way, you create a forum for true exchange and avoid the need for lectures.

How Knowing Nature Makes Your Child People-Smart

Your child's knowledge of his nature will help him to see the nature of others and recognize and accept them for who they are. In other words, he'll learn how to see beyond people's words to the behaviors that reveal them. In addition to making your child people-smart, this is a self-preservation skill that allows your child to recognize those who are dangerous and choose to stay away from them.

To underscore the importance of this skill, let me share a story from my youth. As I was growing up, my family moved all over the country. My father was always getting a new job or being transferred and so, we moved from state to state. Although at most we'd stay in one place a few years at a time, sometimes we moved yearly and once, we moved three times in one year. As a child, this meant being uprooted constantly and having to face the pressures of being the "new girl" and fit into previously established cliques. It also meant that I had no peer support system—no best friend or group of trusted friends with whom to share my troubles.

Although I didn't know it then, some girls were jealous of my status as the "new girl" and would make fun of me to my face or pretend to be my friend and then spread rumors behind my back. Despite my realization that such people were mean, I was raised to be a "nice" girl and thought that there was something wrong with me that made others behave so cruelly. Even though I was smart in school—a straight 'A' student—I was far from being people-smart.

My naivete and lack of understanding of the dark side of human nature caused me needless confusion and suffering. The end result was that I felt bad about myself and afraid of others.

How comforting it would have been to have someone to guide me through those years. A compassionate witness to recognize my pain—to teach me about jealousy and how it steals power by diminishing what is beautiful in others. Someone to teach me how to recognize a person who had the qualities of a true friend and how best to avoid, ignore or devise comebacks for the rest. But I had no such mentor, no lifelong friends and no close extended family because we were always moving. I handled things the only way I could—by taking others' cruelty to heart.

When I look back on some of my childhood experiences, I realize that I want to prevent my children from going through what I did. As such, I've given them a stable home environment and kept a pulse on what's going on with their friends and the kids with whom they have conflicts. While I want my kids to enjoy healthy relationships, I realize that playground taunts and teasing are a fact of growing up and have taught them how to handle it. By helping my children see their nature and know their strengths, the taunts of others are considered for the most part as little more than "background noise." My children are learning that behavior reveals beliefs and values and that a person's actions, rather than his words, looks, smarts, athletic abilities or popularity, reveal his capacity as a friend.

On the occasions when my children's friends have lied or stolen from them, we've talked about how these actions affected the trust in their relationship. This led to conversations about the qualities of a close friendship and how when certain values have been repeatedly violated, it might be time to make a different choice about whom to call a friend. My children are forgiving because like all children, they are resilient, but this is tempered by the knowledge that they cannot allow someone to keep hurting them. In this way, they've learned to separate themselves from others' behavior, establish limits and refuse to be victims.

Although it may make them feel a bit lonely to recognize things that others don't yet see, I'd rather they be lonely, than alone. By knowing themselves and allowing their nature to unfold, they will come to recognize the gifts of others. In this way, they will attract kindred spirits into their lives. This is how our spiritual awareness grows— one heart at a time.

The Gift of Turquoise

By noticing what your child loves to do and giving it a name, you are crystallizing a way of being into a metaphor that your child will use throughout his life to stay connected to his center. In this way, you teach him to create a life that unfolds from strength and give him the courage to be himself.

If you reflect upon all the benefits of naming your child's nature, you'll see that it makes sense to set your child upon the path of purpose from the start. In this way, he avoids the trap of quiet desperation because he comes to know himself and derives joy from the feeling of coherence and harmony this brings. If your child feels good about himself, if he knows who he is and what he loves, then nothing— not people, drugs, money or the temptation of material things—can seduce him from his path.

Like Spirit-Boy in *Spirit-Boy and the Gift of Turquoise,* your child is like a rough-cut piece of turquoise. Your job as caretaker is to polish the stone until it gleams. When its matrix becomes visible, your child will know himself and assume his role as keeper. He will polish it the way you polished him and use his strengths in service of the people.

Chapter 4

Your Child—Your Disciple

*The only world children who have been raised
with compassion and discipline will want to rule
is the inner world: the Kingdom of the Self.*

The True Meaning of Discipline

In order to raise a child, who behaves appropriately and makes healthy choices, you must learn the true meaning of discipline. Unfortunately, many parents and authorities confuse discipline with punishment.

Even some dictionaries fail to make a distinction between the two. In *The New Oxford American Dictionary, discipline* is defined as: "the practice of training people to obey rules, using punishment to correct disobedience." With such a definition, it is no surprise that we have associated child discipline with the tools we use to keep criminals in line: blame, shame and corporeal punishment.

Originally, discipline focused on teaching. In fact, the word *discipline* comes from the Latin word *discipulus*, which means "learner." Before you can discipline a child, he must become your disciple. For this to happen, you must become a leader who is worthy of her following.

A leader leads by example. Her strategies are based on vision, compassion and knowledge of the strengths and limits of her followers. For instance, a parent must recognize that a child is not an adult who understands fully the power of his choices. A child is a student, who is barely beginning to grasp how behavior creates consequences for himself and others. When a child is punished like an adult who has intentionally committed a crime, he identifies himself as being "bad."

Studies have shown that punishing children often *increases* bad behavior. This is one of the reasons parents must learn the true meaning of discipline.

The difference between discipline and punishment is that punishment strives to *teach a lesson* through emotional coercion or physical force, while discipline uses the wisdom of the moment to teach values that show *how* a child can make good choices on his own. A parent who strives to teach her child self-discipline, recognizes her child's growing ability to govern himself. Such parents realize that learning is a process that takes place over time and requires repetition and maturation of consciousness.

There are two aspects of disciplining children that will be covered in this chapter. First, we'll focus on how a parent develops the self-discipline necessary to become a worthy leader. Since most parenting books focus on discipline as it relates to children, this is a new concept for many parents. In looking at how a parent develops greater self-discipline, we will examine the two types of power a parent has and how to choose between them.

The second part of this chapter focuses on teaching children appropriate behaviors. Although this chapter is divided into two parts, disciplining yourself and teaching self-discipline to your child are so interwoven that there is no clear line between them. As such, this chapter goes back and forth between these two important concepts.

The Power of Love vs. the Love of Power

In Chapter 2, we discussed the importance of becoming your child's keeper, until he's ready to keep himself. Although a keeper is a caretaker, he also functions as a guard. A guard's job is to protect something of value or imprison someone against their will.

A loving parent sets her child free a little at a time. Such a parent realizes that even though she's the rule-maker, her child is not a prisoner of her will.

Although you begin your parenting career as the ultimate authority, gradually, you must relinquish authority to your child. Knowing the difference between protection and imprisonment means understanding the difference between two forms of power: the power of love and the love of power.

Like the power of love, the love of power reveals itself through conflict. You might adore your daughter when she's behaving properly, but it's how you treat her when she's misbehaving that reveals your compassion or lack of it.

A couple of years ago, I witnessed a conflict between a mother and her five-year-old daughter that illustrates this point. The daughter had committed a simple act of misbehavior for which the mother berated her. It turned into one of those rants in which phrases like, "you always ..." and "you never ..." were used. While the mother picked apart her daughter, there was an odd glint in her eyes and her mouth twisted at the corners. As she finished her tirade, the five-year-old observed, "You like punishing me, don't you?"

The mother recoiled in horror. Although the cruel smile instantly vanished from her lips, she denied her daughter's revelation: that she used discipline as an opportunity to wield her power, rather than as a tool used lovingly to teach.

Although such a realization would have been painful for any parent, it was an opportunity for this woman to see how her love of power deforms her as a mother.

Children present us with many disquieting glimpses of ourselves, yet they are our kindest and most forgiving teachers. In the beginning, they want nothing more than for us to be with them and wholeheartedly share the wonder of their lives. With their small voices and straightforward way of cutting to the truth, they try to show us how often we push them aside.

Unfortunately, this is exactly what happened between the mother and daughter. Rather than admit the truth, the mother denied what was obvious to her child. In denying the girl's insight, she sacrificed her child. The girl was punished for her recognition of the truth.

What happened here was tragic for the mother and the child. But it was the child who was forced to make the sacrifice. Many parents are unaware of how a denial of reality impacts the consciousness of a growing child. Make no mistake about your power as a parent. Your child will be your sacrificial lamb. A child will give up the truth and her perception of reality in order to preserve her relationship with you. Every time you force your child to sacrifice the truth in order to preserve your ego, you throw a handful of sleep into her eyes.

A few weeks later, I saw this same mother and child again. This time, the child had made a small mistake and was belittling herself out loud. Her mother no longer needed to criticize her because the girl had willingly assumed this role. Her mother's punishing rants had become her self-talk. Better she wound herself, so she would not have to be at the mercy of her mother.

The mother rolled her eyes, as the child continued to belittle herself. When it became tiresome, she exclaimed, "That's enough! You don't need to feel bad about it anymore." The child continued to criticize herself. Finally, the mother sighed, "Who taught you to feel so bad about yourself?" The child hesitated, then pointed her pudgy finger at her mother. Here was yet another opportunity for the mother to see how her love of power had hurt her child, but rather than accept responsibility, she shook her head. "That's not true. You know that's not true." She repeated this several times, until the defeated little girl withdrew her finger.

The mother in this scenario is teaching her daughter to be crazy. Her daughter sees the truth, but the mother demands that she deny it. In order to have her mother's love, she must give up the truth and enter a crazy world where up is down and fantasy is reality. Because this girl must trade truth for "love", she's left with nothing but false security—a mother's lust for power that parades as love—a fragile bond she cannot trust. In order to survive, the girl must secure her mother's love. As such, she lays down her head for slaughter.

Although this may seem overly dramatic, this is how children are drawn into their parents' craziness. This is how they become what M. Scott Peck called "the people of the lie." In his book by the same name, the author explains how inhumane parents manipulate the truth for personal gain at the expense of their children. When children recognize a truth, but the adults in charge deny it, children learn to distrust their senses. Unable to trust themselves, they lose their tenuous foothold in the world. Such children grow up trusting no one. They are lost to the world and lost unto themselves.

This is why it is vitally important to admit your errors. If your child catches you doing something that you're not proud of, apologize and admit that sometimes mommies and daddies make mistakes. Children blurt out the truth, not because they want to hurt us, but because they see it and because they haven't yet learned the social stigma that prohibits them from calling adult hypocrisy by name. A child's world is undistorted by social rules, pecking orders and complex systems of denial.

Children will not enable you or collude in your untruths, unless you coerce them. Take advantage of their insights and learn what is crucial for your growth. In this way, you create room for them to teach you what you need to learn to become a more truthful and loving parent.

Uncovering a Love of Power

America's legal system is based on finding fault. As a product of this system, notice how often you use its weapons of blame, shame and punishment to discipline your child.

To determine whether you've disciplined your child primarily from love or a love of power, observe your child when she's in conflict. A child who has been disciplined with love and patience is less likely to berate herself when she makes an error because she's been taught that mistakes are opportunities to learn.

When you discipline your child, watch for feelings of self-righteousness. Those adults who are quick to blame and shame are often those who most want to avoid catching their reflection in the mirror. If you feel a surge of power when you discipline your kids, examine your motivation. Remember that discipline is not about exercising power over your child. It's about *empowering* your child by teaching him how to make increasingly better choices.

Set expectations for your behavior. Although you're an adult, you are not infallible, nor should you expect yourself to be. Even though you hold a position of authority, you don't know everything. Accept that you will make mistakes and embrace your ability to learn. If you allow yourself to learn, you'll be more patient with your children.

If you're beginning to see how you treat your children like the mother in our scenario, don't dwell on guilty feelings. Use your recognition as the impetus to change. Although it's important to feel remorse because this helps you examine how you can behave differently in the future, it is crucial to move past guilty feelings and make reparations.

How Guilty Parenting Destroys Relationships

In the previous section, we discussed the importance of moving past guilty feelings and making things right. If you steep yourself in guilt, you make yourself into a victim, even though you weren't the person who was harmed. This is a convenient strategy that people use to avoid taking responsibility for their actions. Feeling guilty is not the same as doing what's necessary to make things right. Those who choose to be a victim and mire themselves in guilt do so because it's more comfortable than admitting their mistakes. Instead of righting their wrongs, they feel sorry for themselves. If they condemn themselves, then no one else has the power to condemn them or so they think.

Although the parent who feels guilty in lieu of righting her wrongs might trick her young children into believing that she's sorry for what she's done, as her kids grow older, this strategy will backfire. Older children have little compassion for parents whose guilt is nothing more than a thinly veiled ploy for sympathy. The parent who expresses remorse and works to change to make things right is one who can be forgiven.

There's nothing more annoying than the parent of a grown adult who still feels guilty about how she raised her child, but has not taken responsibility for her actions. Such a parent will often resort to treating her grown child like a little kid in an attempt to cover up her guilt.

To illustrate this point, let me share a story. When my husband was eight years old, his mother sent him to live at a Catholic rectory. At the time, she was a poor, divorced mother of two children. She claimed that she could not afford to feed her son, yet she managed to keep her daughter. Because his mother kept his sister, while she sent him to live with priests, my husband felt abandoned. On the occasions that she visited him in the rectory, he begged her to take him home, but she refused. When he told her that the priests were cruel and physically abusive, she did not believe him. As a grown man reflecting upon his childhood, he said, "I told her that I didn't care that there was no money or nothing to eat. I would have done *anything* to stay with her. *I would have even eaten dirt.*"

These words reveal the pain of a young boy's abandonment by his mother. No matter what the circumstances, the last thing a child wants is to be separated from his family.

To this day, my husband's mother has never offered an explanation or apologized. My husband is in his fifties now and even though it's too late for her to make up for the past, she hovers around him, like he's still the eight-year-old boy whom she abandoned. Her refusal to move beyond her guilty feelings has left her stuck in time, stunted her development and fractured her relationship with her son.

Feeling guilty is self-perpetuating and self-enabling. It's the ultimate in narcissism because it makes everything about you. It's also a convenient way of refusing to confront your inhumanity. If you expect to teach your children discipline, then you must cultivate the self-discipline to look yourself squarely in the eye.

As parents, we will hurt our children from time to time. This is because we're human, we make mistakes, we're learning how to parent and we have unresolved issues from our past. Although these might sound like excuses for inhumane behavior, they are reasons to take responsibility for our growth. This is why it's crucial to become a parent who learns from her mistakes and heals the wounds that she's intentionally or unwittingly inflicted upon her children.

Taking Responsibility for Your Growth

As a parent, you're responsible for all you do, even what you do without awareness. Wait a minute, you say. How can I be responsible for the things I did that I wasn't conscious of? The answer is simple: *you are responsible for your growth.* Like the mother in the previous scenario, when faced with truth, you can deny or take responsibility for it. Although the choice is yours, it has a profound affect on your children.

When you feel bad about how a conflict has unfolded with your child, you have a choice to examine your hand in it. Once you make the choice to see your imperfections, you create another choice: to learn and use this lesson to become a better parent. In this way, your child is the keeper of your personal growth. Although no one talks about parenting at this level, as your child's role model, responsibility for your personal growth is *implied.*

In this chapter, the word "responsibility" is used repeatedly, so it's crucial to understand its meaning. According to the *New Oxford American Dictionary* to be responsible means: "having an obligation to do something, or having control over care for someone, as part of one's job or role." A second definition states that being responsible means: "being the primary cause of something and so able to be blamed or credited for it." Here's the concept of blame again which has nothing to do with the kind of responsibility I'm referring to.

This definition of responsibility leaves out an important aspect of its original meaning. Responsibility equals the "ability to respond" or "responsiveness." According to the dictionary, the word responsive means, "reacting quickly and positively; responding readily with interest or enthusiasm." The word responsive comes from the Latin word *respondere* which is formed from *re-* "again" + *spondere* "to pledge." From this, we will create a new definition of parental responsibility—a parent who is *response-able* responds quickly and positively, *pledging again her interest and enthusiasm for her child.*

This is a definition that beautifully and positively expresses your responsibility to your child. When you examine how you're doing as a parent, this is what you must look at. Do you respond with interest and enthusiasm? In moments of conflict, can you transcend your ego and re-pledge your interest and enthusiasm in order to do what's in the best interest of your child?

In *Spirit-Boy and the Gift of Turquoise*, when Kevote realizes that she is in danger of losing her son forever, she lets go of her defenses and gives Spirit-Boy what he's yearned for all along. Rather than mire herself in guilt about the past, she acts in the best interest of her child. This mends their relationship and rescues Spirit-Boy from the anger that has been destroying him. It gives him the courage to be himself.

Your interest in and enthusiasm for your child create a heightened sense of responsibility or in this case, *responsiveness.* Although you can go through the motions of parenting and resign yourself to duty, you can't fake a genuine interest in your child.

In our society, we're led to believe that parenting is a drudging duty, rather than an opportunity for mutuality and growth. This attitude was instilled in childhood by the way your parents treated you. If your mother saw you as an inconvenience, if she resented rather than celebrated your existence, if she sought to control you, rather than teaching you to be responsible for your choices, then you must take a close look at how you pass these same attitudes to your children.

Responsibility should be less about assigning blame or claiming credit and more about creating a sense of relatedness to those for whom you care. You can do this naturally by letting your children en-*lighten* you and invoke the curiosity and playfulness of youth. Let your interactions with them teach you what you need to learn to increase your skillfulness as a parent. When you respond with genuine interest and enthusiasm for your child, you open yourself to the child in you who is spontaneous and has a genuine desire to give, grow, play at life and learn. This is the place from which a true sense of responsibility springs. Parenting does not have to be a dreary, drudging duty, unless you choose to make it so.

Reflect upon your daily interactions with your child and discover where you can be less rigid or reactive and more caring and humane. To truly take responsibility for your actions, you must become a learner, like your child.

The Reactive Parent

Some parents treat their children harshly and try to make up for it later by showering them with hugs and kisses or unexpected gifts. Such parents often come down hard on children for small acts of misbehavior and turn their heads when their kids act in ways that demand immediate attention.

Parents can be harsh for many reasons. Some parents are overworked with no relief in sight. Others lack an understanding of child development and fail to grasp that their expectations often exceed their child's capabilities. Some parents have a reactive personality that causes them to overreact and take their child's behavior personally. In many cases, this *re*-action is a *re*-enactment of some unresolved childhood conflict between the parent and her parents.

Reactive parents have difficulty responding to a situation because they do not consider their child's level of development. They have difficulty distinguishing between acts committed intentionally and those that were accidental. They fail to understand that learning self-control and how to make good choices is a process and so they punish children as if they were adults. Since these parents use discipline to shame and punish, rather than to teach, their children grow up feeling bad about themselves.

When a reactive father flies into a rage, he lashes out at his children. When the rage has lost its steam, he emerges from it, feeling like he has awakened from a trance. Since the triggers for his rage put him into this trance or fugue state, he may be unable to pinpoint what set him off. Still, he feels bad about his behavior and so, the apologies begin. Unfortunately, since such a parent may fear that an admission of responsibility detracts from his authority, he is less likely to admit his error, than try to make up for it with gifts. Like a wife beater who apologizes with a bouquet of flowers, the reactive parent plays the part of the remorseful dad. Although his remorse may seem sincere, it is not genuine enough to inspire change.

The reactive parent can make things right and gain progressive control of his triggers if he'd own his cruelty, show compassion for those he's wounded, work to heal his pain and engage in the personal growth work required to prevent this behavior in the future. The reactive parent does not realize that he can choose to *respond*, rather than react to those around him. Because he believes that he doesn't have control, he thinks his behavior *happens to him* or that his child provokes his negativity. Since we all have a little bit of the reactive parent in us, it's important to understand this concept. Although I refer to the reactive parent as "he," reactive parents are just as likely to be female. Since women traditionally spend more time with children, it's important to begin to recognize the ways in which we overreact.

What happens to a child who is raised by such a parent? To answer that, let's look at brain research. Jean King, Ph.D., a researcher from the University of Massachusetts Medical School, found that the stresses that occur during childhood can be more damaging than stresses suffered later in life. Since childhood is a time of rapid brain development and stress diminishes blood flow to the brain, excessive stress can change its structure. According to King, "The psychological events that are most deleterious probably occur during infancy and childhood—an unstable home environment, living with an alcoholic parent or any other number of extended crises… What we now believe is that a stress of magnitude occurring when you are young may *permanently rewire* the brain's circuitry, throwing the system askew and leaving it *less able to handle normal, everyday stress.*"

According to Dr. King, stresses that occur during childhood may permanently change how children respond to stress and make it more difficult for them to cope with it later on. Now you can see how reactive parents program their kids to be just like them: hypersensitive to stress. This is how the torch of reactivity is passed from one generation to the next.

In addition to its effects on the brain, stress affects a child's sense of emotional and spiritual well-being, especially when it's inflicted by a parent. The child of a reactive parent lives in a black and white world in which terror and uncertainty reign. Since such parents don't consistently enforce the rules, the child never knows what will set them off. The child tiptoes around these sleeping giants with great anxiety, trying desperately not to awaken them.

The tendency to overreact is compounded by stress. Make no mistake—psychological stress is destructive to our bodies and our relationships. A study published by Duke University concluded that mental stress is more dangerous to the heart than physical stress. Reduce your stress and you will reduce your reactivity. In addition, if you slow down, you will have more time for reflection and begin to see that even during times of crisis, you can choose how you respond.

There are many books on stress reduction. If you are a highly reactive person, here are some basics. Number one: refrain from drinking coffee. Caffeine raises adrenaline levels for hours after drinking it. Adrenaline is a stress hormone that puts your body into fight-or-flight mode. It is my belief that adrenaline triggers the response of our reptilian and mammalian brains, in effect, making us behave like cornered animals. Adrenaline increases levels of a hormone called cortisol. Although cortisol is crucial to our existence, too much of it can actually *shrink* the brain. On the emotional side, it's much more difficult to feel a sense of peace and serenity when your heart is racing from too much caffeine. If the thought of giving up coffee gives you the jitters, promise yourself that you'll try life without it for two weeks. During the first week, you may experience headaches which are caused by increased blood flow to the brain due to caffeine withdrawal. (Increased blood flow is a good thing. It means that your brain cells are getting more nourishment.) During the second week, you'll have the chance to experience the benefit of lower stress levels. Pay close attention to how you interact with your children and others during this period. Notice if you seem more responsive, patient and forgiving. If your relationships and your ability to handle stress improve, you will have a strong reason to give up caffeine permanently. Watch out for hidden caffeine in soda, chocolate and over-the-counter medications.

Eat some protein at every meal. Protein helps balance your insulin levels which normalizes your moods. Refrain from eating processed foods. When you think about providing your body with the fuel it needs to respond positively and effectively, think protein and produce that come directly from the earth.

Drink lots of water. Proper hydration is key to feeling your best. Let the symbolism of water: the ability to go with the flow, let things go and the capacity to take on the shape of its container allow you to experience this aspect of your nature.

Get regular exercise. Moderate exercise reduces stress and gets you out of your head and back into a sense of balance, strength and wholeness. This will help you feel more present, so you'll be less likely to overreact to triggers in your environment. The key is moderation. If you exercise compulsively, you'll create more stress than you relieve. Approach exercise the same way children do: make it fun. Make exercise a family activity with walks, outdoor games and bike rides.

When you feel irritated or angry with your children, recite a simple prayer that was once used by the Essenes to relax the body and create perspective. Repeat to yourself, "Peace in my body, peace in my mind," as many times as you need to let go a little and evoke a feeling of expansiveness. Say these words to yourself *before* you respond to conflict.

Cultivate a sense of humor. Although humor must be used appropriately, it can be effective in deflecting tense situations. For instance, when my son, Dakotah, was four, my husband took him to play football at the park. When he leapt up to catch the ball, it struck him hard on the side of his head. He fell to the grass, screaming and wailing. My husband comforted him, then told him to get up, so they could continue playing and so he could "get back on the horse." My son screamed, "No!" then screeched, accusingly, "You hit me!" My husband, who is particularly adept at using humor, shook his head and smiled, "You're not supposed to catch the football with your ear!" My son smirked in spite of himself and stood up to resume the game.

If you are overwhelmed, learn to ask for help. Delegate tasks to your children that are appropriate to their level of development. In addition to helping them develop a sense of industry and competence, they'll feel good about making a contribution to the family.

If you are serious about overcoming your reactivity, take up meditation. The practice of witnessing thoughts as they arise trains you to be responsive. There is an excellent meditation program that progressively decreases reactivity by using select frequencies to synchronize both hemispheres of the brain. This program which allows you to effortlessly achieve deep levels of meditation is available on CD or tape. To find out more, see the Resources page at the back of this book.

Another way to reduce your reactivity is to make your relationship with your children paramount in your life. Although you have to work to pay the rent, bills and buy essentials, you might not need to spend as much money as you think. Pare down expenditures and simplify. Make your relationship with your child less about giving them things and more about spending time and sharing new experiences. There are plenty of things a family can do for free.

Taking care of yourself, cultivating close, loving relationships and meditating will help you become less reactive. If you still have problems, you may require professional help. Highly reactive people often see the world in terms of black or white. They love you one minute and hate you the next. For such people, there is no middle ground. Such individuals may have a character disorder called borderline personality and should seek the help of a therapist. With time, dedication and the guidance of a professional, the severity of these tendencies can be lessened.

Now that we've examined the reactive parent, let's take a look at the responsive parent.

The Responsive Parent

A responsive parent is one who "**responds again** with **genuine interest** and **enthusiasm** for her child." Everything required to become a responsive parent is contained within this definition.

When your child behaves inappropriately, you must respond immediately in order to help her make corrections to her behavior. For young children, an immediate response is essential because young children are like puppies: unless you catch them in the act of misbehaving, the opportunity for learning has come and gone.

A parent who is responsive understands that appropriate behavior is learned and fine-tuned over time. This speaks to the "respond **again**" part of our definition. In order to teach discipline, you must be willing to repeat yourself and make corrections to your child's behavior again and again. These corrections will range from gross to subtle as your child grasps and refines the concepts. Logical reasons based on humane values need to be given for corrections made.

Some parents respond immediately to acts of misbehavior, while others ignore things until they get out of hand. The difference is between doing what's right versus what's easy. Doing what's right requires an expenditure of time, attention and energy which is a parent's highest expression of love. Parents who are lazy or indifferent will let things slide when it comes time to discipline, unless other adults are present or their child does something that offends them.

When a responsive parent disciplines her son, her intent is to use the situation as an opportunity to teach and empower him to make better choices next time. A responsive parent has no need to blame or shame because she knows that correction leads to self-reflection which fine-tunes behavior over time. This parent knows that teaching discipline lays the foundation for self-discipline, which encourages the child to become self-governing. When a parent's curriculum arises from what's best for the child, she doesn't give up if he doesn't get it right the first time. Such a parent has faith in her child's ability to learn and uses creativity, humor and compassion to reach him.

The responsive parent is committed to self-growth because she knows that she can't discipline her child, unless she is self-disciplined and has conscious control over her impulses and coping styles. Knowing this, the responsive parent challenges herself to become the best person and parent she can be.

Understand that our definition of the responsive parent applies to more than teaching discipline. It is a philosophy that will enhance and deepen every interaction with your child.

A Student of Parenting

When you are hired for a job, you receive training from a person who has experience doing what you are going to do. With parenting, you get your training in the trenches without benefit of a mentor. Unless you've raised children before, you have no idea what you're doing. Even if you have raised a child before, you haven't raised this particular child, so your experience will be different.

Since parenting skills are not taught in school, most likely, you've learned to parent from your parents. Although you may have read other books on parenting, much of your behavior will come from the way your parents interacted with you as a child. Since many parents don't want to be like their parents, they turn to books, but ideas from books don't create new beliefs or behaviors, unless you apply them and make them yours.

If your parents were patient, loving and respectful, then you will treat your children much the same. If you have unresolved childhood conflicts with your parents, then you will tend to have similar issues with your children.

Since most of us had parents who were imperfect human beings, we need to be aware that our children will trigger the re-enactment of significant childhood scenes that still beg to be resolved.

If you understand that your child will trigger your subconscious programming, then you can learn to stop the process with awareness. While some parents will resent their children for the negative traits they seem to bring out in them, this is because they fail to see this as an opportunity for growth. Your child doesn't *make* you annoyed or angry, she brings out in you what is already there. In doing so, she calls forth the beliefs and attitudes that need to be *re*-visioned and the wounds that need to heal.

The parent-child relationship is a dance of mutuality. Although the adult has more experience and maturity, each teaches the other. Parents who are rigid cling hard to the belief in their authority, as though the admission that they don't know it all will expose them as a fraud. In a sense it will because realizing that you don't have all the answers will shatter the mask of authority that protects the ego and stunts self-growth.

Parents who know that they don't know everything will have an easier time of learning and letting go. Since they realize that much of what they have held as true are simply ideas that were swallowed whole in childhood, they know that some of their beliefs are half-truths. As such, they are willing to examine and discard those beliefs that are not in concert with their vision for their child. Such parents identify with their beliefs much less than they do with their desire to give their child the best they can. To them, beliefs are nothing more than lenses through which they have viewed the world. If a lens obscures reality, then it's time to try on a new pair of glasses.

Whatever your child brings out in you belongs to *you*. Take responsibility for your interactions with your child. Inappropriate behavior on your part reveals that you have issues to work on. Becoming aware of this is a step toward positive growth.

It's the responsibility of each generation to heal the wounds and faulty beliefs of the one that came before it. In this way, we choose to discard diseased ideas, rather than pass them on. This is how we raise a generation of children who know that life is about evolution of consciousness.

Since the path of parenting can be challenging, it's important to remember that you are learning as you go. As such, you will make mistakes. There will be times when you'll lose patience, lash out at your children or behave in ways that make you seem like a stranger to yourself. There will be times when you'll wish you could take back the words you've said.

When this happens, be gentle with yourself. Take a moment and breathe into your heart until you experience the expansiveness that allows you to forgive. Rather than feeling guilty, choose to be like Kevote: reflect on your experience, learn, grow and make amends. Forgive yourself and your child will forgive you also.

How Children Learn

Since discipline is about inviting your children to become disciples of your values, then in order to teach them, you must understand how children learn. Although there are many paradigms of learning and cognitive development, the model that best suits our purposes comes from a book by Bill Harris called, *Thresholds of the Mind*. In his book, Bill details the four stages of learning that allow us to incorporate new beliefs and behaviors into our lives.

The Four Stages of Learning:

Unconscious Incompetence—the first stage. In this stage, children don't know the rules and aren't aware that they're not following them. For instance, a two-year-old does not know that his mother will get upset if he throws her purse into the toilet.

Conscious Incompetence—the second stage. At this stage, the child becomes aware of a rule because it's been stated explicitly or because he's been reprimanded. Although he's been informed of the rule, he does not follow it because it hasn't been internalized. For instance, you catch your child dropping toys into the toilet and tell him to stop because the water will ruin his things. Thirty minutes later, he is putting toys in the toilet again. (For a child, toilets are fascinating. There's the splash of the water as he throws in the toy, the bobbing and the floating and the thrill of watching it go bye-bye as it swirls down the drain.)

Conscious Competence—stage three. In this stage, a child can follow the rules, but only when he's warned or reminded by his parents. For instance, you see your child entering the bathroom with a toy and warn him to keep it out of the toilet. He goes to the bathroom without incident.

Unconscious Competence—stage four. In this stage, the child has consciously assimilated the rules and follows them without thinking. He does not have to think about the rules, unless a situation arises that creates a conflict between his desires and values. Your child takes toys and books into the bathroom without needing to be reminded that he mustn't put them in the toilet.

Thresholds of the Mind provides an excellent model of learning because it illustrates the stages through which a child must progress in order to learn a new rule or behavior. A child must go through *four* stages, bridging the unconscious to the conscious and back again, before he "gets" what you are trying to teach.

Contrary to what some parents believe, spanking a child or blaming or shaming him does not speed up the process. In fact, it stunts a child's progress through the stages. As you will learn in another section, disciplining your child by dehumanizing him fails to teach him values.

Read through the four stages of learning again and ask yourself what is most crucial for instilling values and teaching appropriate behaviors. The answers are patience, patience and constant repetition. Teaching requires that you remind your child again and again of what you're trying to teach along with the value of the lesson. Although you'll feel like a broken record, know that each patient reminder nurtures the seed you have planted in his brain. With time, love and patience, the seed will take root and flourish.

Another answer is that teaching values and appropriate behaviors requires creativity and compassion. Children are different—what works for one child will not necessarily work for another. Some children are stubborn. Some are slow learners. Others require creativity or humor. Some have an open mind and will quickly grasp your meaning.

Be creative and find the best way to reach your child. When you're teaching a child to do something, tell him what to do and why. Refrain from making it into a contest of wills by saying, "Because I said so." *Because I said so* is not a reason that makes sense. When you're not around, *because I said so* won't help your child make a healthy choice. If you can't think of a valid reason, then you need to re-examine your rules. By giving your child reasons for why he should choose to behave in a certain way, you're teaching him *how* to reason. This is a skill that he will use to make choices throughout his life.

The reasons you give your child should derive from your family values. For instance, if your child hits another child, don't just tell her not to hit. Squat down to her level and engage her in a brief conversation. Use her hitting episode as an opportunity to teach the value of empathy by asking her how she feels when someone hits her. When she starts to get it, connect the feeling to the action by asking her how she thinks her friend felt when she was hit. In this way, your child will understand why what she did was wrong and why she must apologize. Although words are important, ask her what she can do to make amends. By guiding her through this process, you teach her that people can learn from their mistakes and wrongs can be righted.

It is crucial to understand the process of learning for several important reasons. First and foremost, doing so will set your expectations, so you can muster patience for the child who leaves his dirty underwear on the floor, even though you've reminded him for the fiftieth time to put it in the hamper. The second reason is that this is the same process by which adults learn. Understand this and you will begin to have patience with yourself.

As you learn how to rise above your subconscious programming, you will occasionally act in ways that conflict with your vision. Rather than allowing this to prove that change is impossible, recognize that learning new behaviors is a process that takes time to master. Becoming aware that you've acted from some old belief is better than not realizing it at all. As your awareness expands, you'll make better choices. By learning from your mistakes, you set a family precedent for personal growth. Since learning is a lifetime process, this is a beautiful gift to give your child.

3 R's of Discipline

Discipline should be geared toward teaching children values. Your vision for your child should determine *how* you discipline. Remember that the purpose of discipline is to guide a child to make healthy choices on her own.

Your style of teaching can help your child learn quickly and effectively or can make discipline a nightmare. Following are three qualities to cultivate which will help make discipline a more enjoyable process for all involved.

The 3 R's of Discipline:

Responsive: We talked about being responsive in a previous section. Being responsive means "taking action that re-affirms your genuine interest and enthusiasm in the highest good of your child."

Resourceful: According to the *New Oxford American Dictionary*, the word *resourceful* means "having the ability to find quick and clever ways to overcome difficulties." It originates from the French word *resourdre*: "to rise again or recover."

Resilient: According to the dictionary, the word *resilient* means "able to withstand or recover quickly from difficult conditions." Resilient comes from the Latin verb *resilire*: to "leap back."

When your child makes a poor choice, take it to a higher level. Be responsive by noticing that she's in conflict with a rule or value. Being responsive is an important quality. It means that you care enough to respond immediately and teach your child how to correct mistakes and make things right with others. Being responsive requires that you act with your child's best interests in mind and remember the point of discipline.

If your children whine about "getting in trouble," as my children do, then remind them that you care enough to teach them how to make good choices. When my children complain, my husband and I tell them that it's our job to help them grow up to be good people, instead of jerks. Although we've said this many times, it always elicits a smile.

Being responsive requires that you respond positively to the situation and view it as an opportunity for your child to learn a value or refine his grasp of it. To understand how important it is to be responsive, consider the flip side: parents who fail to respond to their kids at all. Such parents let their kids run wild because they're too lazy, busy or self-involved to enforce the limits. Sadly, the children of such parents will be raised by society: by the school system and later, by the criminal justice system.

Clearly defined limits are an important aspect of discipline. Children want and need limits. Many parents don't realize that children view parental permissiveness as *rejection* because they know intuitively that parents who care, care enough to draw the lines.

Being responsive requires that you re-pledge your interest and enthusiasm for your child each time she goes off course. This requires patience, vision and an understanding of development. (Chapter 6 provides a detailed explanation of human development.) Each time your child gets off track, nudge her back with a reminder of how she's expected to behave and why.

The second "R" of discipline is being resourceful. This means that you find quick and clever ways to teach your children how to make better choices. Being clever might mean coming up with analo-gies or sharing stories from your past. Use humor to reach your child and break up the monotony of discipline. Using humor is also a good way to teach your child to learn from and shrug off his mistakes.

Notice the use of the word "quick" in the definition of resource-ful. Don't turn discipline into an hour-long lecture. State or restate the rule that was broken. Even though you might have stated this rule twenty times before, don't take it personally that your child has forgot-ten it again. Remember the four stages of learning and summon your patient wisdom. Help your child examine the consequences of his behavior and ask him what he's learned. Let him tell you what he's gleaned from his experience in his own words at the level of his com-prehension. Don't correct him, unless he's totally off base. When you allow your child to express his views without correcting him, you get to see how he views the world.

Have faith that eventually, the lesson will become a fixture of his consciousness. Reserve the tendency to rant. If you make each instance of discipline into an opportunity to take out your soapbox, your child will stop listening.

When your children seem unable to grasp a lesson, don't give up on them. Be creative and try another tact. As your kids mature, allow them to make their own mistakes and learn from the conse-quences of their behavior. For instance, my eldest son used to whine when I'd remind him to do his homework. Since he gave me so much grief every time I tried to help him, I decided to allow him to suffer the consequences of turning in a late assignment. This made such an impact on him that he apologized and asked if I would help him make sure he completed his assignments every night. Recognizing his new level of maturity, I showed him how to check himself instead. Now, even though I can count on him to complete his homework, he likes it when we check it together.

The third "R" of good discipline is being resilient. This means that you must be able to recover quickly from what has happened. Once the lesson is finished, move on to something else. Don't hold a grudge. Remember that you are the adult in the situation and it is your responsibility to help your child reconnect with you, so he doesn't feel alienated from you or the family. After a tantrum or difficult situation, I always ask my kids to give me some "heart to heart"—a hug that re-establishes our connection and allows us to begin anew.

When your child acts up, remember that behavior is a momentary choice, not a personality defect. Always focus your words on the action taken: the poor *choice* or inappropriate *behavior*, rather than the child's character. This is important because some children are hypersensitive to criticism which is a good reason to avoid using words like "bad" or even "bad behavior." As I mentioned in Chapter 3, some children are unable to separate their behavior from themselves. Labeling a child as "bad" or labeling his behavior as such may cause him to identify with being bad. For some children, this can be the start of criminal behavior or a lifelong struggle with low self-esteem.

Shaming or punishing your child for dishonesty or any other human trait that you call "bad" is a way to make her assume the label. The strong feelings created during an experience of being shamed can make such an impact on a child that she turns them into a lifelong decision about herself. In that instant, she may decide that her mother is right: she's bad to the core. From that point on, she will *act as though* this were a fact.

When a child gets more attention for inappropriate behavior, than he does for being good, he does what he has to do to get noticed. In this way, too much attention can increase inappropriate behavior. Refrain from making a big fuss about your child's mistakes. If you make discipline about learning how to make good choices, then every error becomes an opportunity to grow.

Make discipline a positive experience in which you teach your child how to think through a variety of situations and deal with the kinds of people that she will encounter throughout her life. If you do your best to teach your child with love and patience and have faith in her ability to learn, she will trust your guidance and continue to seek it, even as an adult.

How the Punishment/Reward System Fails Our Children

In our society, punishment is seen as an effective means of disciplining children. It's presumed that once a child understands that there are consequences for inappropriate behavior, he will learn to think before he acts. In fact, our nation's schools use punishment and reward as an exclusive means of child discipline. If your child misbehaves, he gets a citation or a detention, if he behaves, he gets an "A" for the day, a piece of candy or a sticker.

The idea behind reward and punishment is that behavior which is rewarded will increase, while behavior which is punished will diminish. In theory, this seems sound, but it doesn't always work. As we all know, there are exceptions to the rule: rewards mean nothing to some children and for some, punishment actually increases inappropriate behavior.

The theory that child behavior is driven solely by fear of punishment or desire for reward demeans children's intelligence and fails to acknowledge that they want to do good because it brings them a sense of joy and contribution. In his book *Punished by Rewards*, author Alfie Kohn reminds us that the punishment/reward system equates children with lab rats that will scurry mindlessly through a maze for treats or avoid behavior that results in punishment.

One of the most common criticisms of the punishment/reward system (also called behavior modification) is that it is manipulative. Although you've been led to believe it isn't so, in this system, rewards are just as coercive as punishments. When you dangle something before your child, it matters little whether it's a prize or threat. In the act of dangling, you're attempting to control your child's behavior through external factors, rather than inspiring him from within. When you do this consistently, you teach your child to look outside himself for value and confirmation of his worth.

Controlling your child's behavior is not the same as teaching him how and why he needs to make good choices. While you may argue that dangling a reward is an effective way to prevent a fight or other behaviors that you may find inconvenient or undesirable, the problem is that quick-fix bribes and threats fail to teach children self-discipline or create lasting changes in behavior.

Although this should be enough to convince parents to re-examine their means of discipline, we've barely scratched the surface. If you truly understand the tenets of behavior modification, you will see that it lacks humanity and vision. It treats children collectively, rather than addressing their individual needs. It likens them to robots that can be remote-controlled by authorities, rather than as conscious, willful beings who *want* and *need* to make a difference.

Behavior modification is a science, which lacks an understanding of humanity. It misses entirely the nature of the human spirit and the courage and conviction of the heart. Try as it might, it cannot explain those who transcend their fear of punishment or desire for reward to make choices that serve humanity. This is because behavior modification appeals to the reptilian and mammalian aspects of the brain, while ignoring the frontal cortex and the human heart. Imagine the kind of world we could create if we raised our children to find their value and identity through contribution, rather than reward.

According to Alfie Kohn, studies have shown that rewarding children for good behavior doesn't necessarily increase that behavior or foster a sense of morality. In fact, what ends up happening is that the child learns to value the reward, rather than the act itself. If a father promises his son a toy for helping his grandmother, then the boy fails to learn the value of taking care of those who have cared for him. Since a value has not been internalized, there's no incentive for him to help his grandmother in the future, unless his father bribes him again.

Rewards rob children of the joy of helping others because they distract them from the experience. It's difficult to appreciate the moment when there's a goody dangling before your eyes. The system of reward and punishment keeps our children oriented in the future, rather than centered in the present. It also makes them selfish. When you ask a child who is rewarded for every tiny act to do something, his first concern is: "What do I get?" Behind every spoiled, little brat is the parent who indulged him.

As Kohn points out, while adults are bribing children to reinforce their good behavior, they may fail to recognize that their kids are reinforcing *their* behavior by negotiating increasingly bigger deals. When the rewards get out of hand is when many parents begin to realize their ineffectiveness. By this time, parents may feel they're in too deep—their teenager has become an attorney-in-training, believes that everything in life is negotiable and that every act warrants payment of some kind. The parent who bought his child's compliance has lost it completely. As Kohn points out, it doesn't take a genius to see who has become the lab rat. When you treat children as if they're less than human, *you* become the animal.

Every time you tell your child, "Do this and you'll get that," you're taking the easy way out. While in some situations you might find this necessary, you must learn to recognize the moments in which using bribes and threats sacrifice human values for surface behavior and therefore, shortchange your child. Above all, you must realize that deal-making is nothing more than a way to buy short-term compliance. Children don't grow up to make life-affirming choices on a training program of bribes and threats. Used consistently, behavior modification robs the child of his internal compass and leaves him starving for something he cannot name. In the long run, behavior modification is an ineffective means of teaching child discipline.

Although rewards and punishments do work, they work temporarily and are most effective for two-year-olds and animals. Eventually, like all quick-fix solutions, rewards and punishments backfire. As with junk food diets, quick-fix solutions are insidious and have long-range effects that become apparent later on. For instance, studies have shown that rewards diminish interest and destroy internal motivation. As Kohn says, "Do this and you'll get that, automatically devalues the 'this.'"

Worse yet, many authorities don't realize that children know that adults and teachers are bribing them. Most children are smart enough to figure out that if you have to bribe them to do something, then what you're trying to get them to do must have little merit.

What parents need to realize is that there comes a time in each child's development when bribes and threats do more harm than good. Although this presents a problem for harried parents who have become accustomed to quick solutions, it's not a problem for those who know that teaching children discipline requires time, compassion, patience and faith in children's innate goodness and desire to make a difference in the world.

A More Effective Use of Time-out

In *The Art of War*, Chinese general Sun Tzu states that the best way to win a conflict is to prevent it before it starts. This is excellent advice for parents who strive to teach their children the real meaning of time-out.

When your child *starts* to misbehave is when to put him in time-out. By removing him from a situation *before* it escalates, you help him learn the self-control techniques that will prevent conflicts in the future.

When you send your child to time-out, send him to a quiet room or area, where he will be undistracted by people, toys, television, telephone or video games. The time-out area should be a neutral place that sets the mood for quiet self-reflection. It should have a timer, so your child will know how much time remains before he can resume activity and rejoin family and friends. When our children were little, we used a kitchen timer with a dial. Experts recommend that a child spend one minute in time-out for every year of age. If your child is two or younger, you will have to accompany him and stay with him, until his time is up.

Although many parents see time-out as an ineffective strategy, it is because they view it as punishment, rather than as a way to teach a child to reflect on his behavior. When you are in time-out with your child, avoid physical contact. Tell him firmly that he needs to calm down before he can return to his activity. Show him how to take deep breaths and focus on the heart by breathing along with him. Other than giving these instructions, remain silent while the timer clicks away. Quiet time encourages self-reflection. As your child grows, his early experiences in time-out will have shown him the wisdom of taking a moment to collect himself before responding to a potentially volatile person or situation.

By using time-out as a tool to resolve a conflict before it starts, your child learns to monitor his feelings and be mindful of his self-talk. He'll start to notice when he's about to lose control and will take the time to regain emotional balance. As he learns the art of thinking before he acts, he will grow into an emotionally intelligent, responsive human being.

Practicing Tolerance & Faith

When disciplining your child, it helps to keep the process of how children learn foremost in your mind. To better understand this process, think about a principle that you've been struggling to incorporate into your life. For example, let's say that you want to be more forgiving. How many times have you promised yourself that you would be more forgiving, only to find yourself lashing out or ruminating about people who have done you wrong? Although you understand intellectually that forgiveness frees you from suffering and that a reluctance to forgive harms you more than the unforgiven one, in the heat of the moment, you tend toward self-righteousness. Your tendency to strike back when you've been struck is an animal reflex that requires time, patience, awareness, heart, reflection and commitment to overcome.

Unlike adults, children don't have to break old patterns but like us, they must forge new pathways in their brains in order to incorporate new behaviors. Since children are not jaded and have no old programming, they are quick and eager learners.

Learning is a function of brain development. In human beings, the brain develops quickly from birth until adolescence. As discussed in Chapter 3, humans have four brains: the reptilian (old brain), mammalian (mid-brain), the cerebral and prefrontal cortex (new brain) and the heart. Understand that as your children develop, they will exhibit many of the features that we attribute to the lower brains, such as: pettiness, reactivity and territorial behavior. By teaching your child to positively express his needs and feelings and finding equitable resolutions to conflict, you help him transcend these lower energies so that eventually, he will command the higher capacities of his brain by remembering to engage his heart.

Have faith in your child's ability to learn. Don't give up on your child or she will give up on herself. Find new ways to reach her if other methods fail. Encourage every little step she takes toward a new behavior, just as you applauded her baby steps. Just because your child is no longer a toddler doesn't mean she no longer needs her best supporter at her side. When you temporarily lose faith in her ability to learn, remember that *love is generative of faith*. In the midst of a conflict, focus on your heart, remember something endearing about your child and this will temper your response. Think about your sacred vision and how this moment contains an opportunity to move toward it. Make it a practice to reflect often upon how much you love your child and how she sweetens and deepens your life. Share your appreciation with your child.

Practice tolerance by celebrating your child for who she is and where she is with regard to her development. Recognize how far she's come. When you appreciate her for who she is and how she has grown, you will also become aware of how much *you* have progressed as a person and a parent.

The Perfect Child

Understand that your child is perfect as she is. When you think of the word *perfect*, you probably think of someone who is free from flaws, but this isn't the original meaning of the word. The original translation of *perfect* is "all inclusive" which means "including all the parts." Perfect derives from the Latin word *perfectus* which means "completed" and is synonymous with the idea of *making whole*. Putting these two definitions together somewhat creatively, we'll use *perfect* to mean "making whole by accepting all the parts."

What this meaning suggests is that by practicing all-inclusiveness (which is essentially a tolerant acceptance of your child's feelings, behaviors and character traits), you encourage a sense of wholeness. Tolerance doesn't mean that you let your child behave inappropriately; it means that you accept her outbursts and small cruelties without harsh judgment, then help her make adjustments not to her feelings, but to the ways in which she expresses them.

This concept of child perfection, of *making whole by accepting all the parts* is an integrative function, rather than a divisive one. It seeks to integrate every facet of your child into a whole human being, rather than split off those aspects you find unsavory or annoying. By accepting your child for who he is and how he behaves, you invite him to embrace the full spectrum of his humanity. Since you reject nothing, your child accepts himself and his feelings as a natural part of being human. By teaching him how to channel negative emotions into positive expressions, you show him how to transcend the feelings that we all struggle with. (By *making whole*, you are *making holy*.) In this manner, you gather all the pieces your child presents you with and hand it back to him as an integrated whole. This is how a parent gives a child the courage to be himself.

Practicing all-inclusiveness has benefits for the parent. By recognizing the perfection of your child, you will learn to see it in yourself. In this way, you will gather up all the scattered parts of yourself that you disowned (due to disapproval by parents and authorities) and integrate them into a sense of wholeness.

Learning to *make whole by accepting all the parts* is a practice that opens your heart to all life brings your way. It's the recognition that everything we need for our completion is within us. All we need to do is allow it to unfold. Since all-inclusiveness allows us to fully embrace all aspects of being human, it makes room for new ideas and people of all colors, shapes, sizes, beliefs and dispositions. This is more than a practice of parenthood: it is a practice of *personhood* that will increase your sense of humanity and facilitate the dawning of compassionate awareness.

How Discipline Makes Self-Actualization Possible

When taught with love and vision, discipline teaches *self*-discipline. We've already discussed the meaning of discipline, but what is self-discipline? In *The New Oxford American Dictionary*, "self-discipline" is defined as "the ability to control one's feelings and overcome one's weaknesses" or "the ability to pursue what one thinks is right, despite temptations to abandon it." Proper discipline leads to self-discipline in which the adolescent assumes the parent's role and becomes a disciple of the Self.

Achieving self-discipline is a complex process that begins as a child reflects upon his experiences and sees how his choices create consequences, opportunities and quality of life. From these lessons, the child discovers how to make choices that transcend temptations and are guided by inner strength, so he can pursue the path that feels right to him, regardless of what others say. This is the path that is congruent with his values, his nature and leads deep into his heart. In this way, self-discipline lays the groundwork for self-actualization.

The term "self-actualization" was coined by Maslow in his work on the hierarchy of human needs. A person who is self-actualized fulfills his potential by *real*-izing or "making real" the highest expression of his native talents and capabilities. By developing his highest qualities, this person achieves excellence, personal fulfillment and benefits mankind.

In Chapter 1, you wrote a Sacred Vision for your child. The intention behind this vision is to help you teach your child to know himself, so he can thrive and create a life of meaning and contribution. Your vision helps you focus on your highest intentions for your child, rather than your fears. In this way, your child avoids a life of "quiet desperation" and is set squarely upon the path of purpose. If you've had to grope in the darkness for half a lifetime just to begin to believe that there is such a path, then you will recognize what a gift this is. As caring parents, we strive to give our children better lives than we had because we understand that evolution is their birthright.

The path of self-actualization is the hero's journey. It is the fulfillment of the yearning within each of us to realize our true nature and share our strengths with others. If you have the courage to face your demons, which are really just different guises of the self and if you're willing to take responsibility for your actions, then you can walk this path together with your child.

Start by teaching self-discipline. Self-discipline gives children the tools to pursue their dreams by teaching them that they are *free to choose*, yet *responsible for their choices*. When a child grows up with strong values and learns to value others, he will create a life that benefits him and those around him. Children who are raised with vision will create their lives from vision as adults.

Some parents fear that if they choose to teach, rather than shame and punish their children, their kids will grow up ruleless or worse yet, with an evil urge to rule the world. With few exceptions, tyrants were raised by tyrants who made them into miniatures of themselves.

The only world that children who are raised with love, compassion and discipline will want to rule is the inner world: the Kingdom of the Self.

Chapter 5

Creating Integrity through Humane Values and Conflict Resolution Skills

Children learn what they are shown.

Creating a Family Identity

Family gives your children a sense of belonging. As social creatures, all humans yearn to belong to something bigger than themselves. Throughout childhood, group membership is crucial to the formation of identity.

Children who grow up without a strong sense of family will search for a family of their own. This explains the attraction of gangs and the family-like loyalty that a member expresses for her "homies." In gang speak, your family members are your "homies."

Creating a family identity is an effective way to teach your children values, while establishing a sense of group cohesiveness. In my family, I've created the "Ramirez Family Code of Honor" to define and separate us from the outside world. Adhering to family values creates a sense of belonging, while failing to act from them creates a temporary, but effective sense of isolation. Throughout time, Native American cultures have used the power of group membership to encourage individual members to follow collective mores.

Belonging to a family that has a strong sense of group identity will help your child make life-affirming choices. In this way, a family is no different from a tribe or clan. Even teen gangs have a strong code of behavior, which illustrates that kids *need* clearly defined limits.

In order to define your family identity, a set of behaviors must be codified. When children are young, make the rules few, clear and simple. State the code in positive terms: we take care of people, we take care of property, etc. When rules are broken, state the rule and how it was violated. For example, "In the Ramirez family, we respect our property, so we do not draw on walls." After the rule has been stated, offer an alternative: "Here's a piece of paper and your crayons. Make your picture again for me on paper. When you're done, I'd *love* to hang it on the wall."

When your child is older, you can create a more extensive family code. It's important to record it on paper and post it so it can be referenced easily. At the beginning, review the code often and talk about how its tenets have been followed or disregarded. Acknowledge your child for acting in concert with the code. Remember that the rules must make sense and be based on humane values. If you feel your child is old enough, encourage her to help you write the code. Ask her which values she thinks are most important. When the code has been recorded, discussed and the value of each tenet agreed upon, request that each family member sign and date the document.

Use the outside world to affirm your code of honor. You can use this in many ways, but one way that is helpful is to use people outside the family as examples. For instance, when one of my son's friends stole a game from him, we used this incident to re-affirm our family values. After the friend had apologized and gone back home, I sat down with my children and discussed the incident. I said, "In the Ramirez family, we don't take what isn't ours." The boys agreed that taking the game was a poor choice, but returning it and apologizing were the proper things to do. Using what happens outside the family to solidify core values helps establish a cohesive group identity and encourages your children to learn from what others do.

Creating a Family Code of Honor

Although your family code will most likely arise from your religious and cultural beliefs, I will share some of my values to help you think deeply about your own. While I realize that religion and culture are important aspects of family identity, please make sure that you examine each value carefully before including it in your code. Rather than recording each and every value from your upbringing, make sure to determine first if the value is all-inclusive and humane. As mentioned in Chapter 4, rather than being divisive, all-inclusiveness embraces the whole human being with all his strengths and weaknesses and in doing so, allows for the possibility of growth.

Ramirez Family Code of Honor

1. *Family is first or "Toda la familia!"—everything for the family.*
2. *We are kind to each other.*
3. *People matter more than things.*
4. *We look out for one another.*
5. *We respect person and property and do not take what isn't ours.*
6. *We foster each others' integrity.*
7. *We accept our differences.*
8. *We express our needs and feelings positively.*
9. *We contribute our strengths to the family.*
10. *If something needs to be done, we do it.*
11. *We take responsibility for our actions and make amends when we do harm.*
12. *We are helpful.*
13. *We support and encourage each others' dreams.*
14. *We are forgiving.*
15. *We respect Mother Earth and care for living things.*
16. *We respect our home and property.*
17. *We practice tolerance and give regard to those outside the family circle.*
18. *We resolve conflicts equitably.*
19. *We use love to empower and enlighten.*

When a tenet has been broken, discuss what happened and remind your child of his commitment to the code. Encourage him to make things right by acting in a way that shows his renewed commitment to your family values.

For instance, if your child screams, "I hate you," while throwing an object at his brother, he has violated three codes: "respect for others," "respect for property" and "positively expressing feelings." Wait until he has calmed down and talk about each tenet that was violated. Ask him how he could have expressed his feelings without violence. Help him think of alternatives. Encourage him to apologize and show through his actions how this experience has refined his understanding of the code.

He can show his good intentions by putting back or fixing the item that he threw. Encourage him to do a chore for his brother to make things right.

Teaching Children Honesty

Cultivating honesty in your children is essential to their ability to follow the family code. Honesty is a building block for a healthy relationship with self and others. It is also the cornerstone of integrity. Without honesty, a child will never develop the sense of freedom and imperturbability that comes from living in concert with his heart.

Before we discuss how to encourage truthfulness, let's look at why some children lie. Children younger than five often lie because they have difficulty telling fantasy from reality or because they need to test the waters. This is a function of development and shouldn't be seen as lying. When you ask your child to tell the truth and instead, he gives you fiction, point out the fantasy elements of his story and gently tease out the truth. Remember that one aspect of life that encourages the use of fiction is television. Knowing this, take every opportunity to point out the differences between television shows and reality. For example, when my kids were little and I'd ask for an explanation and instead, get some far-out story, I'd smile and say, "This isn't a cartoon. This is *real life*." With time and patience, they began to know the difference.

Like adults, school age children lie for many reasons. They may lie for personal gain or to avoid punishment or disapproval. They may lie to appear other than they are to gain acceptance by authorities and peers. At the core of every lie is the intention to deceive. Figure out what the child is trying to hide and why and you'll find a way to reach her.

While some children lie occasionally in an attempt to get away with something, others lie habitually. Habitual liars are kids whose parents have not taken the time, care or energy to show them how the truth releases and empowers them. When lying is allowed to continue, it becomes a character style.

Habitual liars often lie in an attempt to cover up what they feel their life is lacking. For children, this may be love, approval, control or safety. Often at home, such children feel that they are loved more for what they *do* than *who they are*. A child should be loved for the fact of her existence. When a child feels that love is contingent upon performance or behavior, she has a strong need to convince herself and others that she is better than she seems.

Although children who lie may seem conniving, remind yourself that you're dealing with a child. Foster compassion by recognizing that habitual liars are borne of fear. They fear that without deception, they'll never be good enough. They fear that without embellishing their achievements or the number of their possessions, other kids won't like them. Since deep down they feel unloved, they must fill their lives with objects that seem to substantiate their worth, which is why they often steal from others.

What these children can't hope to realize is that by lying to cover up a lack of love, approval, control or safety, they create more of what they fear. As long as they lie, no one can know and accept them for who they are because their lies prevent it.

Fear creates more fear. When a child lies to be accepted, she lives in constant terror of exposure and so, must build upon her lies. Until an adult cares enough to intervene, such a child cannot hope to find a way to the truth. When you begin to see the desperation that drives kids to lie, your compassion grows.

Lying begins at home. At one time or another, all of us have been tempted to evade responsibility with a lie. Lies lead to more lies. Lying is like sliding down a slippery slope—once you've started, it's difficult to gain a foothold and stop yourself from tumbling to the bottom. Lying weakens you and hastens your demise. Telling the truth strengthens you and reveals the path that leads back up the mountain. Those who make their way back to the top are rewarded with a big perspective—a privilege that those at the bottom are not afforded.

Honesty begins within the family. It is an essential value because it keeps our children real and connected to themselves, family and others. Honesty makes it possible for children to follow the family code and take responsibility when they have strayed from it.

On the flip side is the child who has become accustomed to getting away with lies. This child has a warped code: her sense of right and wrong depend upon what she wants from a given situation. This child has lied for so long, she may think it is impossible to stop. For such a child, the truth pales in comparison to the drama and excitement that can be built from fantasy.

In order to teach your children to be truthful, *you* must be honest. This means being honest in your interactions with your child, your spouse and others. For instance, if an error is made in your favor, see this as an opportunity to model honesty and return what isn't yours, rather than viewing it as a chance to get away with something or extract payback from some greedy, corporate giant.

Making a commitment to honesty is not a license to tell your children everything, particularly when certain truths are inappropriate for young ears. For instance, when my children ask me the details of subjects that require greater maturity on their part, rather than lie, I say that I am not ready yet to tell them.

Upholding honesty does not mean using the truth to hurt someone. When a nephew asked me if I thought that he was short, I said, "You may be shorter than some of your classmates, but everyone grows at their own rate. This means that one day, you may be taller than the kids who are taller than you now."

Use the truth to open children's minds and create possibilities, rather than limit their perceptions. At the same time, avoid the creation of false hopes.

What to Do When Children Lie

At one time or another, your child will experiment with lying. It is part of development and a normal drive to test the limits to see what she can and can't get away with. Remembering this will help you to avoid taking lies personally.

The fastest way to create a liar is to punish her for lying. Rather than resorting to punishment, focus on what you want to teach—honesty—and give your child opportunities to aspire to it.

The first time I caught my eldest son in a lie, he insisted that he was telling me the truth. Although he was quite convincing, I knew better. I squatted down to his level and asked him to imagine that our hearts were connected by hundreds of tiny threads. "When you lie to me," I said, "you cut one of these threads and sever a connection between our hearts. The more you lie, the more threads you cut. Eventually, lying separates us completely. But when you choose the truth," I said, "those threads grow stronger, until they become impossible to cut." After hearing this, my son said, "Mom, I lied to you. I'm sorry. Can we glue our hearts back together now?" He hugged me and we talked about how good it felt to be honest with each other. In this way, he experienced the release of coming clean with someone whose primary objective was not to shame him, but to teach him how to be true to himself.

Rather than coerce your child into being honest, help him take baby steps toward the truth. In this way, telling the truth helps him to develop a sense of authenticity. Since being authentic will make him feel connected to himself and those he loves, he will *want* to tell the truth.

As a mother, it is my job to keep my son honest, so he can stay honest with himself. I tell him that I understand the temptation of lying because as a child, I experimented with it too. Although initially, I fooled others and tricked myself into believing that I was clever, eventually, I felt like a fraud because the more I lied to others, the more I deceived myself.

Lying hurts the liar because it isolates her from those she loves. When lying is allowed to continue, it becomes a lifestyle that is difficult to stop. "Lifestyle Liars" lie about everything, even little things that do not matter. They even lie about lying, which borders on craziness. Lying hurts the liar more than anyone because it disconnects her from her heart.

How to Help a Child Who Lies

The greatest gift that you can give a child who has a tendency to lie is to present her with a chance to tell the truth. Refrain from humiliating or punishing a child who has told a falsehood or she may cling to it more stubbornly. Instead, give her an opportunity to be honest.

For instance, a teacher discovers that a child has taken another child's toy, but refuses to admit it. The teacher talks to her in private, saying, "Sometimes people lie because they're afraid of being punished, but I promise that I won't punish you for telling me the truth. Other times, people lie because they feel bad or embarrassed about what they did, but it's okay because we are all learning and we all make mistakes. So, tell me… did you take Sara's toy?"

If the child continues to lie, then present her with the evidence. (If you have none, then you'll have to wait until you do. When a child lies about lying, you must confront her with the truth. If she persists when faced with proof, she may require professional help.) Tell her, "I know that you took Sara's toy because I saw it in your desk." Accompany her to the desk and point out the toy. "This is your chance to tell the truth. You'll feel much better once you do and you will not be punished." If the child admits that she has lied, thank her for telling the truth. Tell her how close you feel to her when she is honest. Ask her how it feels to tell the truth. Focus on her sense of relief and reconnection to self and others. Tell her that when we lie to others, we hurt them, but most of all, we hurt ourselves.

The truth heals, but only when we follow up with reparations. When we lie to others, we must admit our error and make amends. Encourage the child to return the toy, apologize and make things right with the other child. Act as a guide to help heal the rift between the children, so each can experience what it feels like to forgive the other for being human.

When a child who has been caught in a lie gains acceptance for telling the truth, her whole world changes. She learns that those who love her care enough to help her be authentic. Such people see her for who she really is: a child, who yearns to feel secure, loved and accepted. This experience will help her choose honesty more often, until she does so without thinking because telling the truth has become a cherished value. Where once she lied to avoid punishment or gain approval, now she can relax in the knowledge that she's okay exactly as she is. Since she knows that all learners make mistakes, she admits her errors readily and grows from each experience. While some kids may like her and some may not, acceptance must come from within. As she learns to accept herself, others will find her more likeable. In this way, honesty is a path back to the Self.

The Parent's Creed

If you want your child to do something, take the time to show her how to do it. Remember that children learn to value what they see their parents do. Although it may seem obvious, this should be the parent's creed with respect to teaching children to follow the family code: *"Children learn what they are shown."*

For example, let's say that one of your family values is: "We keep our house tidy." Rather than order your child to clean up her room, show her how to organize and put away her things. Talk to her while you do it, explaining why you're doing things the way you are. As she grows more proficient, withdraw your help a little at a time. Don't show her once, then abandon her, expecting her to do it on her own. Cleaning a messy room can be so overwhelming to a child that just the thought of it gives rise to frustration, apathy or tears.

Since chores can be a source of conflict in any family, make doing them as pleasant as possible by creating positive associations. When cleaning, turn on music or encourage other family members to pitch in, so it becomes an opportunity to visit while the work is getting done. While our hands are busy, we often share our deepest intimacies. Think of all the heart-to-heart talks you've had while helping your mother wash the dishes or your father fix the car.

When the task is finished, create positive associations with what it *feels* like to have a clean room. Ask, "How does it feel to have a clean room? How does it feel to know exactly where everything is?" Avoid asking questions that require a "yes" or "no" response. For instance, if I asked my boys, "Doesn't it feel better to have a clean room and know where everything is," they will invariably and emphatically answer, "No!"

Although it may seem sexist, most boys have less interest in cleaning and straightening than girls. As the mother of two boys, I've found that a challenge can create some interest. For instance, I'll say, "Let's see if you can straighten that bookshelf in less than eight minutes." To avoid setting them up for failure, make the task doable, but barely. If you have two boys, the other option is to make the task into a fun-spirited competition. There is no prize, save for the pleasure of completion.

Always make sure that the chores you have your children do are appropriate to their level of development. While you can tell your two-year-old to pick up her toy and put it in the toy box, don't expect her to clean up her entire room. Unreasonable expectations set up your child for failure and you for disappointment.

To help your children understand that taking care of property is a value, refrain from rewarding the completion of family chores with money or prizes. Owning property implies taking care of what you own. The reward is in the pride of ownership. Your home should be considered a communal space which means that all occupants must do their part to keep it clean and properly maintained. In our house, we have a rule: If you see something that needs to be done, *do* it. This means rather than walking by a crumpled wrapper on the floor, stoop down, pick it up and throw it in the trash. This is how we take care of each other and keep a home that is reasonably clean and comfortable.

On the flip side, don't expect to have an immaculate home if you have children. If you do, you will drive yourself, your spouse and your children crazy. A home that is comfortable, where everyone can relax is more hospitable and inviting than a home in which everything has to be picture-perfect. Such a home exists only in a magazine or in a compulsive person's mind. In the end, a home will be judged more by what it *feels* like and the quality of the relationships cultivated within, than how it looks. In an appearance-oriented society such as ours, this is a healthy value to pass on. Raise your children in an environment in which imperfection, clutter, and creativity is allowed and you'll raise them to be comfortable with the seeming chaos of existence.

Although we've discussed the parents' creed with regard to the value of keeping a tidy house, understand that this belief applies to everything you teach. *Children learn what they are shown.* Apply this to all you do, from teaching your child how to cope with stress to resolving conflicts with others.

When Values Conflict

While you're teaching your children humane values, you'll run up against other adults and authorities whose behavior directly conflicts with what you are trying to teach. Although this presents a challenge, realize that you will always encounter people whose values differ from your own. You may think that certain adults behave as if they have no values, but everyone operates from a core set of beliefs. Where there is a conflict in values, there is a difference in beliefs.

The word *values* means "principles or standards of behavior." It derives from the Latin word *valere* which means "be worth." How you act (or *be*) reveals what you hold as *worthy*. You discover a person's values by watching what she does. As discussed in Chapter 3, Native Americans learn about an animal by observing its behavior. It works the same with human beings.

As I said before, differences in values indicate differences in belief. For instance, while you may believe in honesty at all costs, your neighbor may believe in honesty only when it serves her interests. Since it's socially unacceptable to admit to such a belief, the only way to discover this is to pay attention to the difference between your neighbor's words and deeds. If you watch and listen carefully, you will discover her beliefs. Once you know that she is honest only when she believes it will get her what she wants, you can determine the boundaries of your relationship. Although it may be fine to share gardening tips, it may be unwise to include her in your inner circle. Whatever you decide, treat your neighbor with regard. To do otherwise is to initiate a conflict. Use what you know to see who she is and make choices about your relationship, rather than condemning her for having different values. When you take the time to understand what kind of "animal" a person is, you won't be shocked by her behavior. Instead, you'll be prepared because you'll know her limits. When we recognize a person's limitations without condemnation, we see them for who they are. In this way, we avoid participating in their dramas.

By seeing people for who they are, we teach our children to do the same. This is an excellent way to avoid a conflict before it starts. When you understand that beliefs create values which determine how we perceive events, you know that different people interpret the same event in different ways. There is no reality, only perception. Although quantum physicists have proven this, humans have a tendency to insist on absolutes. It might help to know that the origin of the word *reality* comes from the Latin *realis* which means "relating to things." Our perception of "the truth" then, has more to do with our values and beliefs. Since beliefs filter what we are able to perceive, people will always see things differently. Accepting this is key to accepting others for who they are and knowing how to deal with them. This creates tolerance which makes conflict resolution possible. If we are to live peacefully with others, we must teach this to our children.

To give you an example of how to resolve a conflict, I'll share a story from my life. Recently, the mother of one of my children's friends called me because her son had traded a card with my youngest son that he later wanted back. Since my son had put the boy's card in a protective sleeve while the other boy had damaged his, my son had refused the trade-back.

Since I realized long ago that trading cards can create problems, I have urged my children to carefully consider their trades. I have also made a rule: if you trade a card, then the trade is permanent, unless the other person agrees to a trade-back.

When the mother of the child called to speak with me, she told me that my son had bent her son's card, but I knew she was mistaken because I had seen both cards before and after the trade. I listened attentively to what she had to say, then told her that my son had refused the trade-back because her son had damaged the card that he now wanted to exchange. When she insisted that he give the card back anyway, I tried to offer a solution, but she hung up on me before I could. Before I heard the dial tone, she made sure I heard her tell her son, "You're never going over there again!"

As I replaced the receiver, I was saddened by her behavior. In particular, I felt sorry for her son because rather than showing him how to resolve a conflict peaceably, she had shown him that friendship is worth *less* than a trading card.

Since I knew that her decision would hurt my children, I took them aside and told them what she had said. When I finished, my eldest son shook his head and exclaimed, "What a baby!" This comment led to a talk about how different families live by different codes and how people's values are revealed through their behavior, regardless of what they claim. I pointed out that this woman's actions seemed to indicate that in her family, *things were more valuable than people*. We talked about how it felt to be on the receiving end of someone who held such a belief. This deepened our commitment to our family code, in particular our belief that *"people matter more than things."*

While this woman's behavior had provided a valuable lesson for us all, I realized that sooner or later her son would want to play with my boys again. Although I could have let it go, I knew that if there was another conflict in the future, she might resort once again to cutting off the children's friendship. Since I couldn't allow her to hold my children at the mercy of her whims, I told my boys that if their friend came to our house, they were to tell him that they couldn't play until his mother called me for a talk. In this way, I extended an invitation to resolve the conflict.

After about two weeks, she called. She made no mention of our previous conversation, so I brought it up. I explained that as caring parents, we couldn't break off the children's friendship just because we disagreed about how a situation should be handled. As adults, it was up to us to show our children how conflicts can be resolved quickly and amicably. She conceded my point and apologized for her behavior.

When I told the boys that the situation had been resolved and their friend could come over and play again, my eldest was surprised. I pointed out that adults are learning too and sometimes do or say things that they regret. If a person admits their error and takes the steps to make things right, we should offer our forgiveness. In this way, we allow people to be human and support their willingness to grow. Since forgiveness is one of our family values, this gave me an opportunity to illustrate it in action.

A few weeks after this incident, I was driving my family to the store. I had the right-of-way and was turning left into an intersection on a green arrow, when a car coming from the opposite direction proceeded into the intersection against the light. At first, I thought the driver would realize her error and stop. When it became apparent that she had no intention of doing so, I was forced to swerve to prevent an accident. When I saw the driver's face, I recognized her as the mother in our scenario.

Later, as I reflected upon this near-collision, I recognized its deeper significance. As adults who have achieved a certain level of maturity, we have to look out for those who are less aware. Knowing this does not give us the right to spiritual arrogance, but makes us responsible for avoiding conflicts with those whose values seem less humane. While we can't force our principles on others, we must recognize their beliefs, so we can act as guardians of the guardians, as discussed in Chapter 2.

A Greater Justice

While the conflict in values described in the previous section was relatively minor, some adults' beliefs may compromise the safety of children. While many adults are wise and caring people, there are those among us who are lacking in judgment or integrity. It is important for children to learn to recognize them, so they can learn to avoid such people.

To give you an example, let me share another story. When my eldest son was four years old, he started taking tae kwon do from a martial arts school. After he turned seven, we transferred to a school in the same chain that was closer to our home. The owner of the school was a master instructor who advertised that his school taught self-defense along with basic tenets of martial arts: integrity, leadership and self-discipline.

One of the first things I noticed about the new school was teenagers taught most of the children's classes and that often, there was no adult supervision, except for the parents who stayed to watch their kids. The other thing I noticed was that there was a lot of goofing off, something that was discouraged at the other school. When my children were humiliated by a series of poor judgments made by the teenagers in charge, I contacted the owner and expressed my concerns. He assured me that steps would be taken to prevent this kind of activity in the future.

One day, after my eldest son had finished class, we were sitting on a bench, watching my youngest son's class. After class was over, the instructor picked up my youngest son and ran with him around the room. He set him down and proceeded to engage in a sparring match. I told my boys to gather up their things because it was time to go. When the instructor saw my eldest son watching from the bench, he challenged him to join them, saying, "Kick me, kick me—I'm made of steel." I repeated that it was time to go. My son stood up and threw a few "promise kicks" (this means kicking at the air to avoid making contact with the other person.) The instructor tried to grab my son's foot and knock him off his feet, but my son was too quick for him. When he finally managed to grab his foot, he threw him back so hard that he knocked my son unconscious.

My son's head injury changed everything. He struggled with behavioral changes, memory loss and headaches for about eight months following the injury. Due to the trauma of being knocked out by a trusted instructor and the problems following his concussion, we stopped attending class temporarily.

When I called the financing company to find out if we could put our monthly payments on hold until my son was ready to return, I found out that the owner had canceled our contract. I called him to find out why he'd done this when it was his policy to make children sign a commitment to obtain their black belts. My eight-year old son had worked hard the past four years and was just two belts away from completion of this goal. The owner became defensive, but in a cool and calculating way. He refused to take responsibility for what had happened. In fact, he called my son a liar, claiming that he had fallen backward on the three-inch thick mat and knocked *himself* unconscious. He accused me of not being there to witness the incident, even though it was he who was not present. I soon realized that talking with this man was pointless.

I share this experience, not to rant, but to point out that things are not always as they seem. As a parent, you might assume that a master instructor who has young children of his own would understand that black belt instructors should not initiate sparring matches after class, especially with children who are not wearing protective gear. You might assume that because the school advertises that it teaches leadership, integrity, and self-discipline that its owner and instructors will model the qualities they claim to teach. If you assumed as I did that appearance equals reality, your children could be forced to pay for your mistake.

As a parent, you can't afford to make assumptions. Check things out. Keep your eyes and ears open. Notice discrepancies. Remember that people have different values. Although someone may have a business that caters to kids, this doesn't mean that they have children's best interests at heart. Adults who truly care for children will understand your concerns and won't be offended by questions or suggestions as to how they can better safeguard the kids. Such people take responsibility when errors in judgment occur. Also, remember what we discussed in Chapter 3: you can tell what kind of "animal" a person is by watching his behavior. Don't be fooled by someone's rank, credentials, polish or presentation: watch what that person does and compare it with the image he projects. It may take time or a particular incident to reveal a person's true motivations. Teach your children this, so they can alert you to signs that you might miss.

This brings up an important point. Although most children are brought up to respect and accept adult authority without question, in some cases, this can prove dangerous or even fatal. As you know, a certain percentage of adults live below the level of integrity. Unfortunately, you won't be able to keep your children safe from all of them because, at some point, they must venture out into the world.

The best way to prepare your children for this eventuality is to indoctrinate them as little as possible. When you raise your children to blindly respect adults, they become easy prey for the predators and less evolved among us. Teach your children that trust and respect are earned, both by children *and* adults. Encourage them to begin any new relationship with a healthy sense of mistrust, which will be discussed in Chapter 6.

During the early part of your children's lives, do your best to surround them with adults who have children's best interests at heart. As your child grows older, support his observations of others and encourage him to trust his instincts. If your child tells you a story about a caretaker that conflicts with what you know about this person, trust your child's perceptions and check it out. With your guidance, your child will learn how to read people as he's growing up, so by the time he goes out into the world, his naivete will have matured into discernment and a recognition of the different "animals" that comprise the human race. In this way, your child will learn to give respect and trust only to those who have earned it.

After my phone conversation with the master instructor, I realized I couldn't talk with him, so I filed a claim with his insurance company for reimbursement of medical costs. Since the owner and the instructor who had hurt my son pointed the finger at us, we soon found ourselves embroiled in a lawsuit. Although I was concerned about how this would impact my son, I thought it was important for him to feel that the justice system would protect him. I also knew that I needed to take a stand against this man and the way he ran his school to decrease the chance that other children might get hurt.

When the case went to arbitration, I discovered the reason why the owner hadn't heeded my original warnings: he had been actively pursuing another career and had his business up for sale. After my son's injury, he sold his business, which meant that he had escaped the consequences of higher insurance premiums. At the arbitration, his credentials garnered great respect from the arbitrator and it was impossible to make his negligence or lack of integrity known. Since the black belt instructor who had injured my son failed to show up for the proceedings, he had no consequences either. Although I was assured that the arbitrator would be impartial, I found out that in his law practice, he specialized as a defense attorney for insurance companies. Perhaps this is why he was more focused on the definition of sparring than the fact that a child's safety had been compromised.

A few days after the proceedings, I awoke in the middle of the night. I was deeply affected by the outcome of the arbitration. It saddened me that although I had done my best to teach my child how to take a stand, the message from the justice system seemed to counter what I had tried to do.

The message was clear: if you lie and hire a bully for an attorney, you can evade responsibility. How could I explain this to my son? How could I prevent this from teaching him that it's smart to lie and that sometimes, the justice system is a sham? How could I teach him to make the right choices when the system had proven that winning at any cost was more important than assuming responsibility for doing harm?

As I pondered these questions, I remembered that a lawyer had once told me that "justice is an umbrella that only covers some." Of course, this definition leaves a lot of people standing in the rain. If I believed that justice was for all, how could I teach this to my son, while acknowledging the outcome? And how could I do this in a manner that did not embitter us?

After some contemplation, I came to this: the justice system was designed by man and therefore, is crude and imperfect. This means that sometimes, innocent people are convicted, while the guilty go free. Weigh your options carefully before entering the justice system because it extracts a heavy toll, especially from the injured party, who bears the burden of proof and the truth of the experience.

Although there might not always be justice in the court system, in the scheme of life, we know there is a greater justice. The true arbiter of justice is life itself.

Native Americans believe that life is a circle. No one escapes the geometry of the circle. What goes around comes around. We are free to choose, but we are not free from our choices.

Although it may seem that a liar has no consequences, it is the choice to lie that prevents him from achieving the level of integrity that creates a true sense of freedom. Instead of knowing what he stands for and acting in concert with those values, he devises a cleverly crafted front. No matter what he seems to get away with or how victorious or smug he seems, the liar sentences himself to life in his self-created prison, unless he opts for change. As Elbert Hubbard once said, "We are not punished *for* our sins, but *by* them."

Although this worked for me, I needed to find a way to explain to my son that actions give rise to consequences, although they might not be readily apparent. To illustrate this, I searched for an analogy, which I'll share with you: some people eat a junk food diet and become obese. Others eat a junk food diet and stay slim, but drop dead of a heart attack one day. Although the heart attack may seem "sudden," the damage has been accumulating for years. While consequences may not always be immediate or obvious, they are at work in the background, setting the stage for the dramas yet to come.

In the end, rather than seek retribution, I chose to find meaning in my experience. Although I believed that my son's head injury could have been prevented, the owner of the school had a different take. Perhaps there was a lesson in this for me as well.

In all fairness, I realized that my intentions weren't entirely pure. I had gone to the arbitration wanting to express my hurt and anger over my son's head injury and the events that followed it. I realized that I had been less committed to resolving the conflict, than expressing my sense of injustice.

Knowing that closure is not always possible, I decided to allow this experience to humble me and offer me a lesson. So I asked myself that oh-so-crucial question: "What can I learn from this?" My search for an answer deepened my commitment to my kids. I realized that, ultimately, *I* was responsible because when I noticed that an authority's basic values differed from mine (most of us will agree that children's safety *is* a basic value), I should have acted as a guardian of the guardians. Rather than be satisfied that I had convinced this man of his responsibility to provide a safe environment for kids, I should have acknowledged his beliefs and found another school.

As caring parents, we make the best choices we can. At the end of the day, it is our choices that define us. While choices are under our control, the outcome isn't up to us. The only facet over which we have control is our willingness to evolve.

The Tricksters among Us

In Chapter 3, we discussed the many types of human animals. This is an excellent way to give your child a basic grasp of human psychology and an understanding of his connection to and place within the natural world. To know a person's animal nature, you observe them, watching closely what they do. Although many people will reject this idea, it is evidenced by the structure of our triune brain: underlying the uniquely human cerebral cortex are the mammalian and reptilian brains.

Although we can't escape our animal tendencies, we can transcend them through spiritual practice, which is the task of a mature adult. Since this is the subject of another book, suffice it to say that there are those among us, whose animal nature isn't tempered much by humane values. Although such people may look like humans, sometimes they don't act like them.

Among us then, are humans who resonate at lower frequencies and can be seen as the reptiles and mammals of the human world. Although we can appreciate the beauty of a wild animal in its element, we wouldn't invite it into our home and we certainly wouldn't leave it in the care of our children.

Although some people have a problem with the classification of others, realize that this is a symbolic self-preservation tactic that will teach your children the basics of human psychology and help ensure their safety. Unfortunately, there are many adults who operate below the level of integrity. While this makes classification necessary, it should also prevent us from turning others into snapshots that we hold static in our minds. Although few choose it, evolution is possible for most everyone.

For easy recognition, you can divide humans into three classes: reptiles, mammals and human beings. To understand the psychology of reptiles, all you have to do is watch them. Since the reptilian brain is responsible for sensory-motor skills and life-sustaining functions, it reacts to food or threats to its survival. Like their counterparts in nature, human reptiles prey on life. These are predators that you want your children to instinctually avoid.

Mammals are a bit more sophisticated. The mammalian brain is responsible for our emotional life and is connected to the heart. Due to this, most human mammals have enough people skills to know how to fool us into believing that they are just like us. Native Americans chose the coyote to symbolize the human animals of this class. In Native American Indian lore, the coyote is the trickster. A trickster is anyone who tricks you either through title, appearances, words or deeds into believing that he's someone that he's not. In the previous section, I detailed an example of a person whom I believe to be a trickster. Although some tricksters are clever, while others are downright dangerous, their common skill is in knowing how to use your feelings to play you against yourself.

In the Native American world, it is a tradition to tell children "coyote stories," so they will begin to recognize the many different types of tricksters in the world. A Karok story, *How Coyote Got His Cunning* which appears in the book, *American Indian Myths and Legends* explains why Coyote must live by his wits, rather than his heart. In the story, the Creator tells the first man to make as many bows and arrows as he can. When he is finished, he is to give "the longest bow and arrow to the animal that he believes should have the most power and the shortest to the one who should have the least." The man gathers the animals together and tells them that he will give out the bows and arrows first thing in the morning with the longest bow going to the first in line and so on. Of course, each animal wants to have the longest bow and arrow. Coyote devises a plan to insure he will get the prize. He props open his eyes with sticks, so he can stay awake all night, be first in line and claim his place as the most powerful animal. After staying awake for hours, Coyote falls asleep. Instead of keeping his eyes propped open, the sticks pierce his eyelids and pin them shut. Next morning, the animals line up, except for Coyote who is fast asleep. The man hands out the bows and arrows and the shortest one remains. When he asks which animal hasn't come to claim his prize, the others point to Coyote. He is awakened and receives his bow and arrow. Since Coyote is the weakest animal of all, the Creator takes pity on him and gives him the cunning that he must rely on to survive.

This is how human coyotes stalk their prey—through appearances and cunning. They are too weak to gain a following any other way. Unwilling to develop themselves through hard work and self-reflection, they resort to tricking others.

A recent example in the media of a trickster is Brian Mitchell, the religious fanatic who kidnapped the Mormon girl, Elizabeth Smart. Since the Mormon faith is known for making its females members into followers, Smart's religious indoctrination made her easy prey. Mitchell, who has the Mormon Bible memorized, brainwashed Smart with her own beliefs and controlled her with such an iron hand that when the Utah police finally found her, she denied her true identity. Wherever there are followers, there's a coyote ready to take the lead.

Coyotes are also prevalent in the media—in the advertisements and infomercials that speak to our insecurities and trick us into buying products we don't really want or need.

Of course, the real coyote is the human ego. In everyday language, the ego has to do with the drives, urges, needs, wants and expectations that determine our behavior. When a coyote promises to satisfy a need, our expectation of its fulfillment is the coyote that often tricks us most.

To teach your children to watch out for the reptiles and coyotes of the human world, instruct them to treat unknown people and acquaintances with *regard*, until they have proven themselves worthy of respect and trust. Although *regard* is used differently today, it originates from the French *regarder*—"to watch" or *re*—"back" + *garder*—"guard." To treat someone with regard means that rather than assume that all people share your values, you must watch your back by observing them carefully. Although this does not give kids license to treat adults with disrespect, it does give them the power to mistrust.

(Mistrust means "minus of trust" and is an important concept that will be covered in Chapter 6.) Had Elizabeth Smart been taught to have regard for others, rather than blind respect for adult authority, she might have found a way to rescue herself from her abductor.

Be aware that there may be coyotes in your inner circle. Over 800,000 American children are kidnapped every year. When a child is abducted more often than not, the perpetrator is a relative, neighbor or someone who knows the family. Take a hard look at the people who comprise your inner circle. If your child doesn't like someone, check that person out. Don't disregard your child because you are afraid of offending an adult. Your child's safety must take precedence over other relationships. Be careful of acquaintances and laborers who have access to your children and your home.

Teaching Children Conflict Resolution Skills

One way to know the difference between human animals and human beings is that human beings express remorse when they have hurt you in some way. They show a willingness to grow by taking responsibility, apologizing, making things right and taking the relationship to a higher level. Their good faith is revealed through actions that foster growth and healing. Since the reptiles and mammals of the human world are guided by their instinct to survive, they have little interest in resolving conflicts. Instead, they do whatever is necessary to defend their territory which reveals their lack of interest in self-growth.

Although there may be no equitable way to resolve conflicts with the human animals of our world, you can learn from your experiences and become more aware of your tendency to be drawn in by their tactics. When you find yourself in a conflict with such a person, an outer resolution may not be possible. True conflict resolution can only occur between human beings who are willing to be truthful and listen to each other.

Conflict resolution paves the way for higher consciousness because it builds bridges between islands. The act of listening creates a bond between the speaker and the listener. It is my belief that this creates new pathways in the brain—after all, this is what occurs as we learn any new behavior. In this way, conflict resolution can be used to foster higher consciousness and should be taught to children at an early age—about the time they enter elementary school.

In the previous section, I talked about my conflict with the owner of a martial arts studio. What my husband and I needed from this man was an acknowledgement of how his negligence had made my son's injury possible. I wanted him to have compassion for our pain and the fear we felt when we were uncertain as to whether our son would recover from his injury. I wanted him to take the actions to make things right and help our son get back into martial arts. I wanted him to rethink his policies about allowing teenagers to teach classes without adult supervision. Basically, I wanted him to care. Much to my dismay, I found myself engaged with an unwilling partner.

In my case, the only resolution possible came from within. To achieve this, I had to forgive this man for defending his territory like a cornered animal, rather than acting like a responsible adult. When I accepted that his behavior revealed his limitations, forgiveness became a possibility.

To forgive means to *"give before."* You *give* compassion to the person who injured you *before* negative feelings infect your life and the lives of your children. Forgiveness means that you accept a person's limits. It doesn't require that you approve of him or invite him back into your life. By forgiving "the animal" for his unconsciousness, we free ourselves, rise above our own animal tendencies and become more humane. (Refrain from allowing the poor choices of another to make you feel morally superior. This leads to spiritual arrogance and is another way of failing to recognize that different people operate from different codes.)

One of the greatest things I learned from my experience with the owner of the martial arts school is how crucial it is to teach conflict resolution skills to kids, so they will practice them as children and refine them as adults. Conflict resolution skills are important because different people live by different values. When a conflict is resolved, each party gains perspective and compassion—two things we need more of in this world.

Before you can teach your children conflict resolution skills, acknowledge that conflict is part of life. If you yell at your children or push them away every time they have an argument, your resistance will prevent you from illustrating how each conflict contains the seed of its resolution. Conflict is a teacher. When two parties learn how to come to a meeting place, they learn that opposing views are different sides of the same coin.

According to *The New Oxford American Dictionary*, the word "conflict" means "a serious disagreement or argument, often protracted." It originates from the Latin verb *confligere* from *con*—"together" + *fligere* "to strike"; the noun is via Latin *conflictus* "a contest."

Conflict arises naturally when two people have different agendas or opinions. Since opinions derive from values, a difference in values is the source from which all conflict springs. Although we cherish our values, many of them come from unexamined beliefs that we swallowed whole in childhood. Some of these beliefs are nothing more than lenses through which we have habitually viewed the world.

In order to come to a resolution, we must turn to the original meaning of the word. From the same dictionary, the derivation of resolution is from the Latin *resolvere*—"loosen or release." In order to resolve a conflict, we *loosen* our position by expressing our needs and *releasing* them as we listen to the needs of others without interruption or argument. In this way, every voice is heard.

For conflict resolution, Native Americans used the circle. In the circle, everyone is equal. There is no first and last. There are no followers. Everyone is a leader because each person leads with her heart. The circle is restorative because it inspires us to wholeness and a greater sense of balance. As we consider the other voices of the circle, we reframe the conflict and our perspective grows.

The Native American 'Talking Stick'

Native Americans use the 'talking stick' in conjunction with the circle as a means of conflict resolution. This is how it works: everyone sits in a circle and when a person wants to speak, she holds the 'talking stick,' while everyone else listens in respectful silence. When the speaker is finished, she passes the talking stick to the person next to her or returns it to the center of the circle. When another speaker wants to express himself, he picks up the stick. This continues until all have said their piece (which often creates a sense of peace).

When a speaker holds the talking stick, he is empowered by the focused attention of the group. In this way, the stick becomes an instrument of open or "I-Thou" dialogue (see Chapter 2) in which one (the "I") listens, while others (the "thou") take turns and speak. By listening attentively until it's your turn to speak, you begin to see how the same event can be interpreted in different ways. (The "thou," which is short for "thousand" can be likened to being receptive to the many voices of the circle.) In this way, we learn how to loosen tightly held positions because each perception has something of value to offer us, if only in opening our hearts to other ways. The circle creates the spaciousness in which this can occur.

Although participation in a circle with a 'talking stick' requires that we listen respectfully, it doesn't mean we must agree. The only requirement is that we show respect by considering the speaker's needs and feelings. Since each person knows that she will have the chance to speak, the desire to argue or defend soon drops away. Instead, there is true communication and sharing. (Listening skills developed in the circle translate into people skills in the outside world.)

In the circle, a resolution is reached when every participant has spoken and the issue has been talked to its completion. When this occurs, the circle expands, creating greater perspective for all.

How to Make a Family 'Talking Stick'

Before you can use the circle for conflict resolution, you need to have a talking stick. Since my young boys are most in need of conflict resolution skills, I sent them on a mission to find a family talking stick. The guidelines for this were simple: the stick must have character, be thick enough so it won't break and be a mutually agreed-upon selection. Sending my boys on an adventure to find something on which they could agree reflected the purpose of the talking stick.

After selecting the stick, each member of the family took it and embellished it in a way that made their mark on it. The only rules were that no one could cover up or alter the expression of another. You can add, but you can't subtract. In this way, the talking stick is an expression of each member and the family as a whole. Since the circle honors every voice, the decorating ritual is emblematic of its purpose.

(This decorating ritual is something that I devised and may not be reflective of Native American culture.)

After your talking stick has been decorated, create a quiet space and present it to the family. When I did this, I told my boys that the talking stick is a sacred tool to use during a conflict that ensures that everyone will have a chance to speak and be listened to with respect. Only by speaking and listening with our hearts can a conflict be resolved.

Like any tool, the talking stick has rules of use. It must be used in a sacred way, only in the circle. When a person is moved to speak, he picks up the talking stick. His statements must start with "I" in order to claim his feelings and opinions as his own and to avoid blaming others. When he is finished speaking, he passes the stick to the person next to him or returns it to the center of the circle. There is no grabbing of the stick. Everyone gets a chance to speak. When it's not your turn, listen attentively even if you disagree with what the person has to say. Focus on listening to the feeling behind the person's words, rather than planning a reply. (In my son's classroom, there is a poster that says, "*Listen* and *silent* are spelled with the same letters." You cannot listen unless you are silent inside.) Try to find points on which you agree. Empathize with the other person's expression of need or pain. When everyone is finished speaking, the talking stick is returned to the center of the circle, followed by a period of silence. After the circle has disbanded, put the talking stick in a special place, until it is needed for another conflict.

Make one of your children responsible for being the keeper of the talking stick. It is this person's job to make sure that the talking stick is reserved for use within the circle. This person may suggest its use for conflict resolution or for coming to mutual decisions. Since each child should have a chance to be the keeper, you can rotate this responsibility between family members.

Make sure that everyone understands the rules of the circle. In the circle, all participants are equal. To become a leader, you simply speak what's in your heart. If you feel anger, express it using an "I" statement, then let it go as you pass the stick to others and focus on what they have to say. While a speaker holds the talking stick, others must be silent. You may not speak until you hold the stick.

Once a circle has been formed, it can't be broken until all speakers have finished and all have observed the period of silence at the end. By giving ourselves fully to the circle, we let go of defensiveness, so healing can occur.

Facilitating Conflict Resolution

Story is an effective means of helping children imagine how new tools and rituals can change their lives. Since children identify with the characters and situations in a story, it opens their eyes to new ways of being in the world. Although children are naturally receptive, a good story engages and inspires them, causing them to re-imagine themselves.

With regard to teaching children conflict resolution skills, this is crucial because kids who are used to fighting to make themselves be heard will have a hard time giving up the surge of power generated by an indignant outburst versus the quiet energy required to resolve things peaceably. As we all know, there are certain people who feed off conflict—they need it to make them feel alive. Interestingly enough, the word "indignant" comes from the Latin *indignant*—"regarding as unworthy." Implicit in righteous indignation then is the assumption that the other is unworthy of being treated in a calm and respectful manner. In any situation in which a child must first give up his power in order to be empowered, story is helpful because it inspires, rather than coerces.

In *Tales from the Dragon's Cave*, author Arlene Williams offers a collection of stories that will inspire your children to learn how to resolve conflicts peacefully. One of the stories, "The Dragon Stick" comes from the author's experiences as part of a group in which the talking stick was used to resolve conflicts and come to a consensus on important issues. Since the main character in the story is one of mythic imagination—a dragon—children are captivated immediately. The story itself is a moving and often humorous tale of how four antagonistic brothers use a talking stick to learn to resolve their problems. Through the use of the talking stick, they learn to listen and see each other as beings with needs and feelings, rather than objects on which to vent their anger and frustration.

When I read "The Dragon Stick" to my children, I did so in our backyard. It was a beautiful spring evening of gathering twilight, with hummingbirds hovering nearby, sipping nectar from the flowers in our rock garden, while crickets chirped in the background. Reading my children this magical story amidst the drape of approaching darkness added potency to its message. The boys instantly grasped the purpose of the talking stick. When I told them that they were to go on a mission to find our family talking stick, they jumped up with excitement.

The next day, after they had found the talking stick, the much-anticipated demonstration began. After the power of the circle and talking stick were illustrated, each member was invited to decorate the stick in their own way. Since they already had a meaningful experience, they took the time to embellish it in a personal manner.

When conflicts are resolved peacefully, everyone benefits because each party gains greater awareness and compassion. Using the Native American talking stick in your home will teach your child to speak his heart and listen compassionately to others. The talking stick used in conjunction with the circle teaches children diplomacy skills and helps them see what lies beyond a difference in values—another human being.

Chapter 6

The Nature of Evolution

*The difference between your child's ability to thrive
or 'just survive' is you.*

Understanding Child Development

The need to teach parents the basics of child development became clear to me when I heard about a father who beat his two year old daughter to death after she failed to "properly" clean up her room. Although this is an extreme example, all parents can benefit from an understanding of human development. Since most parents are not taught this subject in school, we will explore it in detail. If you don't grasp the concepts right away, keep reading—it will all come together in the end.

Understanding child development is important because it helps you set realistic expectations for your child's behavior and give her tasks which challenge, yet do not overwhelm her. The successful completion of each developmental stage builds a firm foundation for the next. If you are aware of the struggles presented by each stage, then you'll know how to use them to help your child gain a growing sense of competence.

There are many theories of child development, but we will use Erik Erikson's model which was developed in his book, *Life Cycles*. Erikson's theory is appropriate because although he was a white man, he observed Native Americans to develop it. He spent two years living with the Yurok and Lakota tribes, recording parent-child interactions. Perhaps this is why his theory is spiritually based and includes more than just the stages from birth to adolescence. As its name implies, Erikson's theory of development encompasses the entire life cycle because the capacity for human growth spans the time from birth to death.

Understanding that development is a lifetime process creates meaning and gives perspective to our struggles. Since the path of human development is one that we all must walk, an understanding of the process creates a sense of connection to and empathy for others.

Erik Erikson called his developmental stages "life cycles" because although we progress through them in a series, if a conflict presented at a certain stage is left unresolved, it affects the next stage and becomes a recurring theme. To some degree, though, certain issues will resurface. For example, the first stage of Erikson's model is *trust vs. mistrust*. As a child, you trusted your mother, but at age twelve, your parents divorced, your father remarried and you gained a step-mother. Since you had to determine whether to trust or mistrust this "second mother," you had to go through the process again to some degree.

According to Erikson, each stage of development presents a crisis between two opposites, as in *trust vs. mistrust*. The crisis is resolved by finding a sense of balance between the two. A balance—knowing whom to trust and whom to mistrust creates a sense of optimism and gives the child growing faith in his powers of discernment. As a child successfully completes the tasks required of each stage, he earns what Erikson calls a "virtue" or a "strength." Without this strength, growth is stunted at the current level of development.

Although Erik Erikson is credited with his theory of development, he created it together with his wife, Joan. Her idea that a person's progression through the stages can be symbolized as a weaving is detailed in her insightful book, *Wisdom and the Senses*. Using this metaphor, throughout our development, we weave together the opposing elements of each stage into a tapestry that reveals our beliefs about the world. To create a vibrant tapestry, we must learn to balance life's seeming opposites.

As we mature into adults, this requires that we refrain from taking either/or positions. It means that we walk the fine line between opposites, which allows us to accept the spectrum of humanity with all its gradations. When we embrace the paradox, we enter the realm of greater truth. This is the meaning behind the Native American saying, "Walk in balance."

In *Life Cycles*, Erik Erikson defines eight stages or "ages" that describe the transitions that are universal to us all. Since the premise of this book is that the parent-child relationship is one of *mutuality*—as the parent encourages the child's development, the child inspires the evolution of the parent—I will include the later stages to help you understand the entire process of human development from birth to death.

Trust vs. Mistrust

The first stage in Erikson's Life Cycles theory of development is *trust vs. mistrust.* This includes the years from birth to the first or second birthday. Since establishing trust is essential to creating healthy relationships, this section is long and detailed. In it, I repeat myself intentionally because I want to emphasize the importance of this time.

During this stage, if a child's cries are responded to with love and consistency, then he comes to trust that they will be met the same way in the future. This sense of trust is the child's first experience of *relationship* and the model for all that follow. When a child's needs are attended to sporadically or not at all, he develops a basic mistrust in his caretakers that translates into a mistrust of human beings.

In her book, *Wisdom and the Senses*, Joan Erikson states that she considers "basic trust and mistrust 'necessary contraries' for life can only be faced with a potentially trusting outlook and yet cannot be lived without some adaptive mistrust to ensure survival." Although mistrust is a 'necessary contrary,' the parent-child relationship must lean heavily toward the side of trust.

According to Erikson, trust vs. mistrust encompasses much more than the physical. For instance, to provide sustenance, to make eye contact, to care for, to cuddle and caress engages the child on all levels of his being: the physical, emotional, mental and spiritual. This is "bonding" which is the key to healthy relationships and the gateway to higher consciousness.

There is a difference between the parent who only picks up a child when he's crying and the parent who actively engages the infant, who plays peek-a-boo, who gazes lovingly into his eyes and delights in every minute detail of his progress. Such a parent celebrates the child for the mere fact of his existence. This creates a sense of trust that extends beyond that which is created when a parent focuses only on a child's physical needs.

A parent who attends to her child only when he makes demands of her is acting from a sense of duty, while a parent who engages her child emotionally does so out of genuine affection. To the developing child, the differences are striking.

According to Erikson, children are born into the world with their senses ready for stimulation. While inside the womb, they have the capacity to hear, taste and open their eyes. Since the fetus lives *inside* the mother, it is likely that he absorbs her thoughts and feelings as his own. From this we can surmise that in actuality, the experience of *trust vs. mistrust* begins in the womb. A child's sense of trust or mistrust depends on how a mother feeds her body and the emotional climate she creates for the fetus with feelings about her pregnancy and impending motherhood.

Since a child is born with his senses intact, he's primed to bask in a parental affection that celebrates him for the fact of his existence. When a child's birth is met with reluctance, indifference or resentment, although he cannot name it, he feels this too.

Birth is a passage from known to unknown. The womb, which is the child's planet and atmosphere, anticipates and provides for every need as it is expressed. The womb is fluid and responsive. Unfortunately, when the baby emerges from it, its owner may not treat him with the same regard.

When my children were born, I knew that birth was an important passage, but I also saw it as a painful separation. The fetus is pushed from a warm, comforting, known environment into the great unknown: a world of harsh lights and sounds. The baby who as a fetus had every need provided for must find a way to get his needs met because he knows instinctively that he cannot meet them on his own. At first, the only thing he can do is cry. If his cries are met with reluctance, hostility or indifference, he learns right off that he must fight for his survival. If his cries are met with compassion, comfort and the quelling of his need, he feels relaxed and secure. An atmosphere of safety creates the inner calm required for a child to *thrive* in his environment. The difference between a child who is given the opportunity to thrive and the child who must fight to survive is like night and day. *Early experiences with primary caregivers form the lens through which the child creates his self-perceptions and his beliefs about the world.*

When my eldest son was born, rather than reading a slew of parenting books, I took my direction from the womb. After all, it had been the first "mother" to my fetus. I took the placenta home from the hospital and buried it in my garden. (This is a common practice among indigenous people.) The placenta had served us well and I thought it proper to return it to the Earth. As I buried it, I reflected upon the womb and its qualities—a warm, comforting, fluid, stimulating, highly responsive environment. If those qualities were what allowed my child to thrive inside me, then I knew that they would help him thrive in the outside world as well. Although I loved the sweet intimacy of motherhood, I realized that each step of my child's development would take him away from me, so I decided to let him determine when and how these separations occurred.

During his first year, my son and I were constant companions. I carried him with me everywhere I went. I did household chores one-handed. I even held him while I sat at the computer and wrote articles. My child slept with my husband and I every night until he was two years old, nestled between the warm, safe pillars of his parents' bodies. When he cried, I responded instantly because I was right beside him. I did not let him cry himself to sleep: I rocked him or snuggled him until he nodded off. When he was ready, we bought him a toddler bed and he slept at the foot of ours. A year later, he moved into his own room.

When my second child was born, my eldest was so secure in my love for him that he welcomed this new baby with open arms. Experience had assured him that there was enough love for everyone. During this time, I was finishing up my B.A. in psychology, so I had many responsibilities, in addition to being a mother. My second son was born in the middle of the semester, as I worked toward my masters in creative writing.

The key to a positive outcome for *trust vs. mistrust* is to take your cues from Nature. As explained above, I used the qualities of the womb as a guide to teach myself how to be a mother. I trusted the unfolding of my child's development and allowed him to indicate through his actions when he was ready to take small steps of independence. By listening to the nature of my womb and its fruit—the child—I achieved a sense of balance as a mother. In this way, I allowed myself

143

to die a metaphorical death and was transformed from a self-involved individual into a mother. I gave up many of my preconceived notions about parenting and trusted in the wisdom of something bigger than myself—Nature—*and* something smaller than myself—the child. This became a huge leaping-off point for my spiritual growth. I thank my children for this opportunity every day.

Erikson points out that although mothers and fathers do the best they can, it may not be possible to meet an infant's every demand. For instance, my eldest son cried every time I handed him to my husband, but there were times when I could not hold him or take him with me. I remember once when I had to take a test at school and gave the baby to my husband to watch while I was gone. As soon as I handed him over, he began to wail. When I returned two hours later, I could hear him screaming as I emerged from my car and walked up the pathway to the house. When I opened the door, he jerked his head toward me and sighed with great relief, "Ma… ma!" He was six months old at the time and the word he had uttered was his first. One glance at my husband's face told me that our son had screamed the entire time I was gone.

While it's important to do your best to meet your baby's needs, there will be times when you'll have to leave him in the care of someone outside the family. Although you'll want to make sure this is someone you trust, this will allow your child to experience trust and mistrust along a small continuum that is critical to his future ability to determine whom to trust.

The elements of trust and mistrust are equally important because achieving balance is made possible only through the experience of opposites. In order to thrive, your child must eventually develop the capacity for discernment: she must learn whom to trust and whom to mistrust. (Discernment comes from the Latin *discernere: dis* "apart" + *cernere* "to separate" which means to perceive or know. What judgment seeks to condemn, discernment seeks to recognize.)

If an older child is stuck at either end of the *trust vs. mistrust* continuum, her view of others becomes maladaptive. For instance, if a child is too trusting, she may discount intuitions about potentially dangerous people and situations. If a child trusts no one, then she will close her heart to all. Since a baby or toddler doesn't have the capability to make decisions about whom to trust, you must carefully screen those who provide her care.

As the child grows, the theme of *trust vs. mistrust* continues to be an influence. For instance, the twelve year old who trusts everyone leaves herself open to being victimized, while the child who trusts no one shifts into survival mode, avoiding people and doing everything in her power to stay "safe." Although these kids are on opposite sides of the spectrum, neither achieves the sense of balance necessary to thrive.

In order to emphasize that a successful resolution of each stage of development is achieved by a continual balancing of opposites, I have taken Erikson's developmental scales and adapted them by adding a concept called the 'thrive-survival' continuum. The 'thrive point' or 'balance point' is located somewhere in the middle. In the case of *trust vs. mistrust*, the balance point indicates that the child has bonded to his caretaker and achieved a sense of trust. Since the child has a true caretaker, he has a "safe harbor" to return to when he encounters someone he mistrusts. These brief forays into the real world reveal the gradients of trust and give him an accurate picture of the kinds of people he will encounter in the world. As he grows, he develops the ability to discern between those he can trust, those he can't and those he can trust with certain things. By contrast, the child who mistrusts his primary caretakers has little chance of experiencing what it feels like to trust someone outside the family home.

A loving mother-child bond is crucial to the development of trust because it allows a child to experience "mother" and those who are "not mother." These experiences create a basis for comparison and help the child to develop a new strength. In the case of *trust vs. mistrust*, the strength is "hope."

A child who achieves a sense of hope knows that no matter who he encounters, he has a safe harbor to return to. Since he notices the differences in response that he gets from mother and those who are "not mother," he develops an internal sense about in whom to place his trust. As he grows older, he develops the ability to shift between trust and mistrust as he sees how different people behave and notices the discrepancies between what they say and do. Such a child can trust and mistrust in proportions that are reasonable given those involved, their history and the particulars of the situation. In actuality, there is no one "thrive point," since this is a sliding scale that shifts its weight along a continuum as the child encounters different types of people.

In order for a child to arrive at the thrive-point, he must be able to trust that his primary caregiver will exert a positive counter pull that will center him after he has encountered authorities he cannot trust or trust as fully as his parents. As he matures, his parents will act as a sounding board and teach him how to put others' behavior in perspective. This is where the Native American practice of "knowing the animal by watching its behavior" becomes particularly helpful.

At opposite ends, are the "survival points"—where certain children tip the scales, depending upon whether they trust too much or not at all. When a child tips the scales, he is out of balance and sees the world in black-and-white. Rather than living fully, this child is barely getting by. He becomes a victim or a survivor, but not a "thriver."

Another important point about the thrive-survival scale is that the word *survival* is a noun, while *thrive* is a verb. A noun indicates stasis—something that is fixed and stagnant. As a verb, "thrive" is an action or a state of being and indicates that a child is evolving—learning first the gross and then the finer points of balance. (The ability to make increasingly fine distinctions is considered a hallmark of a genius.) For instance, the child who has made a decision to trust no one may give up on people entirely. In this way, he "fixes" his perceptions to protect himself which means that no one can "move" him or help him change his mind. Since *trust vs. mistrust* is a recurring theme, this is a decision that can last a lifetime.

The New Oxford American Dictionary defines *survival* as "the state or fact of continuing to exist in spite of an accident, ordeal or difficult circumstances." Its derivation is interesting because it comes from the Latin word *supervivere*, which means "to live in addition to." The question that arises is: if you are living in addition to or in spite of something, how fully are you living?

From the same dictionary, the word "thrive" means "to grow or prosper" and comes from the Old Norse word *thrifask*, which means "to grasp or get a hold of." So while surviving implies *getting by* despite some trauma or difficulty, thriving means "getting a grasp on something" or as I like to put it: "using insight and reflection to make increasingly fine distinctions." In this way, achieving the "thrive point" causes the child to actively engage and balance opposing concepts in a way that eventually reveals the paradox and all its permutations. I call this process "striving to thrive."

Trust vs. Mistrust

<u>Survival</u>----------------------<u>Thrive</u>--------------------<u>Survival</u>

Too Trusting--------------------Hope-------------------Withdrawal

Here is the thrive-survival scale for *trust vs. mistrust*. Remembering it is a scale of balance and counterbalance, you see that according to Erikson, when a healthy child encounters someone new, she starts off somewhere in the middle because she does not yet know whether she can reasonably trust or mistrust this person. Her experiences with the person will be weighed against her experiences with her primary caretaker in order to come to a decision. What this means is that *you* are your child's reference point. *Your relationship with her is critical to her future ability to trust, form healthy relationships and make accurate discernments about others.*

To understand the meaning of trust, we must know its opposite. The prefix "mis" in the word "mistrust" comes from the Latin word: *minus.* To be mistrustful of someone is to be *minus of trust.* This is different from *distrust* because the prefix *dis* implies a reversal and means that you trusted someone whom you no longer trust. In this way, being mistrustful of someone you do not know is both people-smart and healthy. You are open to trust or mistrust, until insight derived from your encounters tells you which way to turn. If it's in the direction of trust, then you give this person a little at a time and watch what they do with it. You do not tell a new acquaintance all the secrets of your past and "trust" them to keep it confidential. This is false trust and is nothing more than a personal dump. People who are prone to this are those whose scales are weighted so heavily toward mistrust that they give their hearts away to strangers to confirm the core belief that there's no one they can trust.

In order to encourage a flexible "thrive point" in your child, you must first provide him with an experience of what trust feels like. You must be the person on whom he can consistently rely for his physical, emotional, mental and spiritual needs.

A few years back, I wrote an article for my online newsletter which can be viewed by going to www.parenting-child-development.com. In this article, I describe the failure to love a child as a breach of the most basic trust. Love and trust are elements of the sacred contract between parent and child—a contract that is implied from the moment of conception. When you create a relationship with your child that is based on trust, you are preparing her to thrive. If instead, you offer her experiences of mistrust, she will have little hope to experience its opposite in the world.

When your child knows that she can rely on you, she experiences trust and uses this to discern whether to trust, mistrust or distrust those who come into her life. A child who emerges from this first stage of development with a healthy balance of *trust vs. mistrust,* has a sense of hope. As she grows, this sense of hope will make it possible for her to create healthy relationships with others and gain confidence in her powers of discernment.

Autonomy vs. Shame and Doubt

The next stage in Erikson's theory of development is *autonomy vs. shame and doubt* and extends from one to about three years of age. As a child develops physical control, such as learning to control his sphincter muscles, he learns the art of holding versus letting go. Parallel to this is his emotional need to balance the comfort of mommy with his drive to explore what lies beyond her in the outside world.

As your child expresses his alternating need to be comforted with his drive for independence, you are learning to hold on and let go as well. During this stage, look for cues from your child to tell you what to do. It's not appropriate to smother a child, while he's striving for independence, nor is it appropriate to turn away a child who is crying out for comfort. Parents who are overly controlling or who live vicariously through their children will tend to stifle their child's sense of autonomy, thus tipping the scales toward a sense of shame and doubt. If a parent does not allow a child to struggle when doing so is age-appropriate, the child will learn to doubt his capabilities. For instance, it's appropriate to allow a one year old child to struggle to climb up on the couch, rather than giving him a boost up every time. In this way, he gains confidence in his ability to strive toward what he wants.

Using Erikson's model in combination with the thrive-survival scale, we have:

Autonomy vs. Shame and Doubt

Survival------------------Thrive------------------Survival

Willfulness----------------Will------------------Compulsion

Over-confident----------Will------------------Doubtful

Shameless---------------Will----------------Shameful

In Chapter Four, I wrote extensively on the negative effects of shame and blame in disciplining children, so I will not elaborate further here. The important thing to know is that there's a difference between the shame imposed on a child by a parent and the internal feeling of shame that naturally arises when a child realizes that he's made a poor choice. The use of shame must be avoided because it is not a tool of discipline, but a weapon of self-righteousness. Externally imposed shame compounds a child's natural shame in a way that is damaging. Discipline should never be used to belittle a child, but to lift a child's emotional awareness to a higher level.

Autonomy vs. shame and doubt is also a stage of learning to identify and let go of or hold onto feelings, which means it is a crucial part of your child's emotional development.

According to Joan Erikson, since this is the stage when a child first exerts his independence and leaves the mommy-home-base for moments at a time, this is when children first feel their parent's fear or anger when they stray too far away. At this stage, a child needs a sense of autonomy counterbalanced by self-doubt, so he will venture from the mommy-base, but not too far. He needs a healthy sense of internal shame, so he knows when he has exceeded other people's limits. These feelings will naturally arise in him; he does not need shame or doubt imposed on him from without.

During this stage, you must closely watch your child as she ventures into the unknown. The words and feelings of the parent are soaked up by the child and form her self-perceptions and inner dialogue.

If a child ventures too close to the edge of a landing and the parent screams, "No! You'll fall," the parent has given the child a vision of herself tumbling down the stairs. Make your child aware of dangers, rather than afraid of them. Choose to be proactive, rather than reactive. Recognize that due to the nature of curiosity, your child will naturally gravitate toward the edge. Knowing this, take your child's hand and accompany her there, pointing out that she must be careful in places where it's possible to fall. In doing so, the child learns to explore her environment with care. Since she's been shown the possibilities in a manner that is not startling, her will is tempered by an awareness that will guide and protect her as her confidence and physical abilities grow.

The 'thrive point' of *autonomy vs. shame and doubt* is "will." A child's will develops guided by the opposing tensions of doubt and willfulness and internal shame and shamelessness. In this way, the child learns to direct her will positively in a way that includes a growing assessment of her capabilities, a respect for her limits and that of those around her.

Initiative vs. Guilt

Initiative vs. guilt encompasses the years from three to five and is characterized by a playful exploration of the world. During this stage, children should be encouraged to use their skills of fantasy, drama and imagination, to discover the world fully through their senses and run, spin, climb and jump to increase balance and coordination, while a responsible adult looks on. Group play teaches children social skills and how to cooperate with others. During this time of exploratory play, the child ventures further from the mommy-base.

Beneath all this whirling, bouncing, jarring activity is the purpose of play. While the parent's job is to take care of and provide for others, the child's job is to play. Although compared to a parent's responsibilities, a child's task may seem relatively unimportant, it is crucial to healthy development. Through play the child begins to understand relationships, the world and his place in it. Through play, the child develops initiative, creativity and a sense of purpose.

When my boys were this age, my husband in all his wisdom

used to tell them that deep inside each of them was a man and deep inside him was a little boy. As a dad, it was his job to bring out the man in them and as children, it was their job to help him remember how to play like a little boy. In this way, he enlivened their play with a sense of purpose, which further inspired them and meant we had boys jumping at us from all directions.

When you emphasize what your young child teaches you, you create a sense of mutuality. In this way, parents can teach and children can remind us. Each has something of value to give the other. Parents instill a sense of responsibility and purpose, while children inspire and enlighten us with their joyful spontaneity.

According to Erikson, if play is restricted at this stage or if a child is shamed for the joy he feels in expressing his physical capabilities, he may become immobilized by guilt and inhibited by the harsh judgments of his parents. This may cause him to withdraw from his peers and lose his desire to engage in imaginative physical play. Ripped from his childhood in this way, he may remain dependent upon adults, rather than growing through an exploration of the world.

If a child is encouraged to play and use his imagination, yet taught to respect that other people have limits for noises and jarring activity, then he learns when playfulness is appropriate. This is the thrive-point for *initiative vs. guilt*—an active sense of physicality and imagination that engages others in cooperative play, yet recognizes that there is also a time and place for stillness. According to Erikson, a child who has not been permitted to fully explore his physical abilities tips the scales by feeling guilty or inhibited and may bully others who exhibit joy in relationships and play. At the opposite end of the scale, a child whose playfulness is unrestrained may stubbornly demand that everything be turned into a game that is centered on his enjoyment. In this way, he exhibits a ruthless disregard for the limits of others.

Initiative vs. Guilt

Survival-----------------Thrive-----------------Survival

Ruthlessness--------------Purpose-----------------Inhibition

Industry vs. Inferiority

This stage encompasses the early years of education from about age six to twelve. During this stage, a child is faced with learning new skills at home and school. If he perceives himself as having more successes than failures, he will develop a sense of confidence in his ability to learn. If he has more failures than successes, he may believe he is inferior or incapable of learning.

This stage of the game is about learning, not mastery. A child must learn *how to learn* and develop a feeling of confidence in his ability to comprehend anything to which he applies sufficient effort. This is why I feel that during this stage, there should be no letter grades in school. Grades separate students into categories, such as: "brains," "average-joes" and "failures." This is a time when many children are at risk for assuming labels that others place on them or giving up entirely. Poor grades assist in this determination. In my opinion, the focus of this time should be on fostering the joy of learning and discovery, the power of imaginative inquiry and the individual passions that burn inside each child.

The strength that emerges from a successful resolution of this stage is a sense of competence: the belief that with practice and persistence and the help of others, a child can learn anything.

Industry vs. Inferiority

Survival--------------------Thrive-----------------Survival

Narrow-Virtuosity--------Competence------------------Inertia

As mentioned previously, I believe that these years should be focused on inspiring passionate inquiry and learning *how* to learn. I remind my children all the time that like life, school is about learning and growing. It doesn't matter if they get a "C" on a test, as long as they learn from their mistakes. While I don't expect straight A's, I expect my children to illustrate a willingness to correct themselves and grow. This can be difficult in school situations in which the primary goal is high grades and test scores. Learning should be fun and does not need to be based on competition. Where there is competition, there will be winners and losers. When it comes to a child's self-perceptions, this is a dangerous game to play. If a child loses too often, his passionate flame for learning can be doused. For some children, this creates a lifetime struggle with a feeling of incompetence.

When my eldest son was four years old, he took classes at a martial arts studio, where the students participated in competitive drills. The children were divided into four teams and had to race against each other. I remember watching my son, who was the smallest and the last runner for his group. As he darted across the finish line, his teammates roared in victory. When the noise died down, the eldest boy on his team taunted a member of another team: "We won, we won! You lost!" My son tugged the older boy's sleeve and said, "It's not about winning... it's about learning." Now, as a nine-year-old who thrives in the competitive environment of little league sports, I often have to remind him of what he knew when he was four.

When parents put too much emphasis on grades or performance, a child may develop performance anxiety because she feels her whole identity is at stake. Children who are pressured to get high marks no matter what, learn to study for the grade, rather than the joy of learning. Good grades arise naturally from interest. Interest is inspired by excellence in teaching and parenting—by teachers and parents who find creative ways to fan a child's inner flame. If curiosity and interest aren't dampened by a focus on rewards, a child will carry her passionate pursuit of learning like a torch that lights her way through life. With regard to learning, the means and ends must be the same. A child who is taught to perform tricks for treats: studying hard solely to be rewarded with the external "A" and the approval of authorities, develops what Erikson termed a "narrow virtuosity" and sacrifices the joy of discovery for a letter grade.

When this happens, the externally motivated child learns how to do what must be done to get the "A." I understand this from the inside out because I was a straight "A" student. I was raised in a family in which I was expected to get all A's. The expectation was so high that I was nervous before and during tests. I suffered from performance anxiety because my whole identity revolved around getting a high mark. As a student, I learned how to give my teachers what they wanted: in many cases, just a word-for-word regurgitation of what they had taught in class. Although I don't blame the teachers, I was also smart enough to recognize how my ability to parrot their lessons gratified them.

In this way, I carved out an identity as a straight "A" student and teacher's pet. Although I was convinced I had everyone fooled, I didn't realize that the only person I was tricking was myself. Instead, of grasping concepts and learning how to apply them to my life, I studied for the tests and became a master of mimicry. In this way, I sacrificed the creative for the literal. Looking back, I see this as the death of my childlike curiosity and wonder. Although I knew how to get perfect test scores, I couldn't think for myself. This is the danger of raising children to base their self-worth on external measures like grades and test scores.

A child who is encouraged to follow his passionate interests will naturally excel. He may do better in some subjects than others, but his enthusiasm will reveal his natural proclivities and spur him on to achievements that are inspired from within. Although this child may be pleased that his efforts are acknowledged by society, he will accept awards with humility because his sense of vitality, competence and purpose remain independent of such measures.

Identity vs. Identity Confusion

This stage characterizes the period of adolescence which lasts from approximately twelve to twenty-one years old. It is a confusing time for most children and calls for great compassion and sensitivity on the part of parents and authorities.

Identity vs. Identity Confusion

Survival-----------------Thrive-----------------Survival

Fanaticism---------------Fidelity-------------Repudiation

The thrive-point of *identity vs. identity confusion* is fidelity, which means faithfulness to oneself and a growing congruence between values and actions. Tipping the balance at either end, we have fanaticism and repudiation. According to Erikson, fanaticism refers to a position taken with excessive zeal, while repudiation involves a denial of everything one has cherished.

The key to this stage of development is helping your child have faith in her spiritual sense of self. This is especially important during a time when your child's identity is enmeshed with the beliefs and assumptions she has adopted from you. During this highly stressful phase, she tries to disentangle herself from you to discover who she is, what she believes in and what she wants to do with her life.

According to Erikson, the answers to these questions may not be obvious or they may come too quickly. This is why in the Native American culture, this is the time of the Vision Quest. The goal of the Vision Quest is for the young adult to seek a vision of herself that will guide her through the turbulence ahead and lead to a life of her own making. While a teenager may profess to know exactly what she wants to do as an adult, Erikson advises that it is best to encourage her to take advantage of these last years of childhood to explore the many avenues available for her expression. If a child identifies too much with certain ideas or aspects of her identity, she risks becoming a fanatic and/or being drawn into a cult. If she remains confused about her identity, she's at risk of rejecting herself and everything that has held a place of meaning in her life, including parents, family, friends, and culture.

This is a critical time in parent-child relationships since the child's outright rejection of the parent may be perceived as a personal affront. It's crucial for you to see this as a normal part of child development and avoid taking your teenager's moodiness or criticisms to heart. To help, recall how you behaved toward your parents when you were a teenager. If you grew up in a strict home where such expressions were forbidden, then remember how you felt.

Know that in order to find himself, your child may temporarily try beliefs and roles that are in direct opposition to your own. Since the primary task of this stage is for the child to disentangle from the parents, understand that your child may need to reject you in order to find himself. Celebrate your child's attempts at self-discovery, as long as they are not injurious to him or others. Smile and know that your child stands at the cusp of adulthood.

As I mentioned earlier, the key to a successful transition

through this stage is to help the child stay connected to his spiritual sense of self. This sense of self transcends all social roles and is realized through the unfolding of his nature. In Chapter 3, we talked about the importance of giving your child a spiritual name. If a teenager has been grounded in his nature since childhood and his parents and extended family have lovingly encouraged him to seek what is in his heart, then he will have little to rebel against because he will have embraced his uniqueness all along. The significance of having a spiritual name will become apparent to your child in his darkest hour, when peer pressure threatens to seduce him and create conflicts between values and free choice.

Your child's knowledge of his nature reveals his strengths which give him three important ways by which to thrive during adolescence. First, a knowledge of his nature and its uniqueness give him a sense of self-worth. This sets him apart from his peers and teaches him to trust and follow his own lead. Second, knowledge of his strengths gives him a means of being faithful to himself. This encourages him to take actions that are congruent with his values. Experiencing himself as strong, he naturally selects people and ideas that strengthen, rather than weaken him. Third, his strengths offer him a means of acceptance by his peers. Rather than mimicking others to fit into the crowd, his strengths give him a means of *belonging through contribution.* In this way, he gains acceptance by his peers *and* remains faithful to himself. Empowered by his strengths, this teenager emerges from the labyrinth of adolescence as a *man*, who has a strong sense of self-fidelity and a desire to be of service to the world. This man diverges from the well-worn path and cuts a trail toward self-actualization.

Intimacy vs. Isolation

This stage describes early adulthood and includes the years from approximately twenty-one to forty years old. During *intimacy vs. isolation,* adults learn how to create mature relationships based on varying degrees of intimacy. We talked about intimacy in Chapter 2. Remember that intimacy refers to more than the physical closeness experienced in sexual relationships or marriage. It also refers to the emotional kinship that is experienced between friends or between a child and parent.

Intimacy vs. Isolation

Survival------------------Thrive------------------Survival

Promiscuity-----------------Love-----------------Exclusivity

A person who is afraid of emotional commitment can only experience intimacy via casual sex. But the need for intimacy runs deeper than sexual experiences can provide and so for the promiscuous, satisfaction is fleeting. Those who cannot achieve emotional intimacy risk a sense of isolation and self-absorption. As Joan Erikson notes, although some people devote the energies of this stage to a cause, rather than a person, this exclusivity may be motivated more by a fear of intimacy than a higher choice.

A person who is unafraid of true intimacy can love another with respect, tolerance and commitment. A person who can be emotionally intimate with another has first learned to be intimate with the self. Here again, we see the hand of nature. An adult who has grown up knowing his nature and faithfully expressing his strengths, can see others because he can separate who he is from who he isn't. Rather than projecting his hopes and expectations on another, he is able to see and accept the other person for their weaknesses and strengths.

Since a person who knows his nature is intrinsically focused, he doesn't demand that others meet the needs that can only be met by following the heart. This person knows that mature love is based on want, rather than need. Since such a person's dependency needs were met during childhood and since his parents raised him to be self-sufficient, he wants a wife with whom he can share his life, rather than a mother figure who will coddle him like a child. In the same way, a woman wants a man with whom she can co-create a life, a home and a family, rather than someone who will play daddy to her inner little girl.

When two people who know and respect each other's nature come together, they create a love that is based on spiritual equality and recognition of each other's strengths. The thrive-point for such a couple is intimate love. In intimate love, one loves the other for who that person is and encourages their unfolding. When a person is able

157

to love the self and others, he has the foundation for a happy marriage, enduring friendships, fulfilling parent-child relationships and successful partnerships in business.

Generativity vs. Stagnation

Generativity vs. stagnation extends from approximately forty years old to sixty. Although I've discussed the concept of "generativity" in a previous section, we'll start with Erikson's definition: "generativity" involves concern for society and future generations. The danger with this definition is that some elders will equate "concern" with "worry." To make things clear, we will define generativity as acting in a way that gives to others. During this stage, well-adjusted elders use the wisdom accumulated during a lifetime to contribute to their family and society at-large.

The virtue or thrive-point of this stage is "care." For instance, a parent in this stage will take her love for children and give to others by donating time to a children's cause or charity or through other means that extend her energy beyond the family circle.

As a person who has been writing and publishing articles on the internet for free for the last six years, I know that generativity is more than the obligation to pay back a debt to life: it is the desire to give for the sake of giving. When giving arises from a genuine desire to share your strengths with others, rather than a sense of duty or obligation, it creates a higher level of service. The ability to give without reward or reciprocity comes from the ability to love maturely that was fostered in the previous stage. In this way, love is a progression: from the love of self, to the love of family and friends to the love of community and finally, to humanity at-large. In this way, our elders have the ability to love more fully than at any other stage of life.

As Erikson points out in her book, there are many adults who cannot give beyond their inner circle because they're part of what we call the "sandwich generation" and are busy raising children, holding down a job and taking care of aging parents. Understand that caring for family members of different generations also creates a sense of generativity. For those who don't have the time or energy to give outside their circle, the virtue of care can be expressed at home.

According to Erikson, an adult who is unable to care for those inside her inner circle may feel stagnant, develop extreme dissatisfaction with life and blame those around her. This can lead to marital discord, infidelities or some other type of mid-life crisis. But stagnation can also lead to growth, as when a person realizes that time is running out and decides to pursue a lifelong dream. Such a person may give up a job that provides security for a career that expresses deeper aspects of her nature.

Generativity vs. Stagnation

<u>Survival</u>------------------<u>Thrive</u>------------------<u>Survival</u>

Over-extension----------------Care--------------------Rejectivity

At either end of the thrive-survival scale is the person who gives too much. We are all aware of the woman who gives without replenishing herself. Such a person will wake up one day and discover that she's compromised her health. Often times, such people turn to stimulants. Refuse to rely on stimulants. Find a balance of work and play that rejuvenates you physically, emotionally, mentally and spiritually. Draw firm limits. Give with joy when you feel inspired and able to do so.

Integrity vs. Despair

Integrity vs. despair is the final stage of life that extends from age sixty to your deathbed which was the starting point for this book. Recall that in Chapter 1, I asked you to create a deathbed vision. When you're finished with this section, you'll understand why every heartfelt vision must begin at the end.

In *integrity vs. despair*, Erikson defines the word *integrity* as a person's ability to accept her life and take responsibility for how she has lived it. Integrity comes from the Latin *integer* which means "intact." When you have accepted yourself and your life choices, you can love those around you in a deeper and more meaningful way. In this manner, you claim your life in its entirety and extend the sense of generativity that was developed in the previous stage. As you progress through the later stages of development, you'll have more compassion for those who are struggling through earlier stages. If and when they ask for it, you can offer your perspective and act as a kind and loving guide.

According to Erikson, at one end of the scale, we have presumption. Unfortunately, old age does not equal wisdom. There are plenty of elders, who use the number of their years as justification for their "right" to give unsolicited advice when their intent is to offer nothing more than harsh morality or judgment. Dispensing unwelcome advice can hardly be considered compassionate or giving.

Integrity vs. Despair

Survival------------------Thrive------------------Survival

Presumption---------------Wisdom--------------------Disdain

In her book, *Wisdom and the Senses*, Joan Erikson states:

> "Our first basic strength, you may remember, was *hope*, the Latin source being the verb *sperare*, to hope. How appropriate then, to find our form of this word *desperare* as the final dystonic element with which the aging individual must cope. Desperation and hopelessness have usually been the accepted lot of the "sere and withered leaf." How then shall we command the kind of tensile strength which physical disintegration and loss contribute to the last years of life?"

Although despair is usually perceived as a negative, it is important to embrace it. As energy wanes and the body begins to fail, we are made keenly aware that the physical is the vehicle through which the spirit descends and knows itself. In this way, despair assists in your transcendence, creating the dynamic tension that pulls you back to the thrive-point, so you can accept your physical demise with integrity and grace. This is your cue to share the wisdom accumulated during a lifetime to those to whom you pass the torch.

According to Erikson, what prevents you from tumbling into the trap of disdain or presumption is an acceptance of how you have lived your life with all its twists, turns and choices: good and bad. Unfortunately, in this linear time-based, cause-and-effect world, there is no way to change the past, but perhaps therein lies our grace. The only way to create change is by moving forward. The only way to "take back" is to give. In this way, the power of this stage lies in using what we have gleaned from life to make further contributions. For elders who have achieved integrity at this stage, it may be insulting to suggest that they spend their final years in retirement. Instead, life offers them another chance to give. This is how wisdom fades, like the final flower before an endless winter, its dying breath a waft of fragrance for us all.

Eros, Thanatos and the Thrive-Point

In Greek mythology, Eros was the god of Love. In psychology, eros refers to our drive toward life and all that supports it. By contrast, thanatos, refers to the death instinct which is signified by suicide, withdrawal, rejection or slow disintegration. In the thrive-survival scale of Erikson's cycles of human development, the thrive-point is associated with an integration of seeming opposites and the ability to discern between and balance them in order to sustain life and foster growth. The survival-points are associated with beliefs borne of trauma or misperception which throw a person off-balance and compel him toward self-destruction. If you grasp one thing in this chapter, know this: the difference between your child's ability to thrive or just survive (at least initially) is *you*.

Helping your child achieve a sense of balance is a goal of which many parents may suspect that they fall short. Realize that achieving balance is an ideal. It is difficult to keep an eye on your child's development when life has knocked you flat. Many things can happen to temporarily remove your focus from your child: the death of a loved one, an illness or accident, the break-up of a relationship or the loss of a job. When you realize that you've been distracted, return your focus to your child.

Now that you have a map of human development, you can see how each stage builds upon the next. *Hope* clears the space in which *Will* can play. *Will* creates *Purpose*. *Purpose* inspires *Competence*.

Competence generates *Fidelity* to the self. *Self-fidelity* makes it possible to *Love* another. *Love* and the sense of mutuality created by raising a family give birth to *Care* for family, community and humanity at-large. *Care* ripens into *Wisdom* which gives to others and raises awareness through its presence. This is the evolution of human consciousness. *It is your birthright and the birthright of every child.*

If you think back to the Sacred Vision that you developed in Chapter 1, you will recognize that your deepest yearning for your child must include humanity's highest virtues. Where there is vision, children flourish. If you study this chapter and use your interactions with your child as opportunities to encourage the development of the strengths of each stage, your child will grow into an adult whose life is guided by nature, virtue and an inextinguishable love of life.

Choosing to Become a Humane Being

Although we are all born human, we must *aspire* to be humane. To make the word *human* into *humane*, you add an "e," but to shift from a human into a human**e** being requires a transformation. The fact of your birth makes you human. *To become humane, you must give birth to yourself.*

The famous psychiatrist, Viktor Frankl once said, "The spiritual is what is human in man." This is true in part. In order to balance lower animal "survival energies" like fear, shame and ruthlessness, we must accept them as part of the experience of being human. Understanding human development connects us with others because it is a path that we all must walk. Once you see this, you realize that your child's growth is intertwined with yours. His development contains the seeds of your *becoming*. It is who you *become* while raising your child and working toward your sacred vision that will make you into an exceptional human being. The spiritual is what is human**e** in man. That "e" makes all the difference in the world.

According to *The New Oxford American Dictionary*, a *human being* is "a man, woman or child of the species *Homo sapiens*, distinguished from other animals by superior mental development, powers of articulation, speech and upright stance." Although this defines us by our physical capabilities and differentiates us from animals, what distinguishes

162

humans from humane beings is *how* we wield our power.

To act humanely is to act with mercy, compassion, tolerance and vision. This is what is spiritual in man. Whenever possible, those who act humanely use their power to *empower*, rather than to force. Using power to empower is a relatively new concept in parenting that flies in the face of what our parents knew and practiced. Despite this, we must strive to evolve past the limits of our upbringing and offer the children the highest in ourselves.

The Leaping-Off Point

In human development, each level is the starting point for the next. In much the same way, you are the leaping-off point for your child's evolution, just as your parents were the starting-point for yours. By taking full responsibility for who you are and how you raise your children, your offspring will *spring off* to a higher level of adult consciousness.

This is the essence of parenting and what I refer to as "intergenerational evolution"—what occurs when the preceding generation endows its heirs with the tools to create more fulfilling lives.

Human beings are capable of raising the bar in terms of consciousness, conservation, love, tolerance, humanity and compassion. Parents must do their best to help their children create fulfilling lives, but many parents confuse this notion with giving children better parties, more expensive toys, exciting outings and vacations. Although your child may look forward to such things, teach her that while external things may bring a temporary sense of happiness, lasting joy comes from within.

Before we return to the subject of intergenerational evolution, let's take a look at the meaning of the word. *Generation* means "all the people born and living at about the same time, the production of something or a single stage of development." The root of the word is *generate* which means "to reproduce." Although your child is the product of the physical union between you and your partner, in emotional, mental and spiritual terms, your child's level of awareness is *the sum product of your level of evolution.*

Your stage of development is the starting point from which your child begins his journey. You are the springboard to his *becoming* because until he begins to question his assumptions, he views himself and the world through your beliefs. Through your daily example, he learns how to be an adult, a parent, friend, part of a couple and how to treat himself and others. When you realize that in raising a child, you are raising your great grandchildren, you begin to understand the level of vision to which you must aspire.

The word *generation* is related to the concept of *generativity* that was discussed earlier in this chapter. According to Joan Erikson, *generativity* means "generating in every sense of the word—procreating, productivity, creativity—through an investment of one's capacities in the generation(s) to follow." Although for most parents this is a busy time of life, the key to the stage of generativity is "to care for" that which you have produced or in the case of children, those whom you have reproduced. Remember that caring for a child means tending to his physical, emotional, mental and spiritual needs which requires taking the time to know his heart.

Since this period of life asks much of you, it's important to recognize that during this stage, you are learning *how* to parent and *how to care for* someone other than yourself. The demands on you are endless because as you are learning, your child is growing and developing which changes what you have learned. Know that the upheaval caused by this constant change spurs *your* growth. Although the surface rules keep changing as your child matures, the unspoken promise of a parent—*to care for and be there for*—must be your constant vow.

During this time of learning, be gentle on yourself and recognize that the myth of perfect parenting is just a myth. If you allow yourself to learn from your mistakes, you will accommodate your growth. If you believe that you must be the ultimate authority who is never wrong, your rigidity will stunt your development and fracture your relationship with your child.

As the springboard of your child's *becoming*, your level of awakening is the level at which your child begins to comprehend the world and his place in it. This means that you are responsible for the lessons you pass on. Know that your beliefs, attitudes, coping styles, etc. will be soaked up by that super-absorbent sponge that is your child's subconscious mind. Take responsibility for what you teach by making parenting an important aspect of your growth.

In his book *Man's Search for Ultimate Meaning*, psychiatrist Viktor Frankl points out that it is not man who asks the meaning of life; it is life that asks the question of man. This means that life has no meaning other than what you assign to it. In other words, it is personal. It is up to you to find meaning in your relationship with your child.

Parenting requires working on yourself, so you can plant seeds in your child's subconscious mind with vision of the fruit such seeds will bear. If you don't examine your beliefs and are sowing seeds simply because they were sown in you, then although your parenting skills may lack intention, you are still accountable for what you have sown.

You are *free to* choose, but you are not *free from* your choices. You are responsible for every action, whether you think it through or not. This requires that you become aware of what you've given birth to in yourself *and* in your child, even if it was passed down to you by those who came before.

How can you be expected to take responsibility for things that were below your level of awareness? By committing to your growth. By seeing your mistakes as opportunities to learn. By carefully considering the beliefs and coping styles that you pass on. By recognizing that every seed you plant in your child's fertile garden mind has the sustenance to sprout. When you notice seedlings that were planted unconsciously, thin them out by replacing them with the seeds of conscious change.

As a parent in this stage of development called "generativity," all your efforts must be geared toward teaching your child *to care*—to care for the self, the Earth, the community and for each strand in the intricate web of life. Although you may be distracted by your varied responsibilities during this busy time, make a commitment to refocus again and again on what it means to be a parent to your child.

Chapter 7

Teaching Your Child to Thrive in a World of Surface Charms

Integrity is the true measure of self-worth.

Creating Healthy Relationships

Your relationship with your child provides the model for her relationships with others. Through your interactions, your child learns how she can expect to be treated and how she should treat others.

The New Oxford American Dictionary defines "relationship" as "the state of being connected or the way people are connected." The root of the word is *relate* which comes from Latin *relat*—"brought back," from the verb *referre*—"to bring back." In this way, our relationships with others return us to ourselves. Relationships are recursive because they reveal how we feel about different facets of ourselves.

How you relate to your child is how you relate to the child in you. Understanding this is key in creating a loving relationship with your children. Parents who shame or severely punish their children are operating from old beliefs that were instilled in them by their parents. You can stop this vicious cycle by owning the ways in which you pass on what was passed to you. One way to do this is to use your Sacred Vision as a guide for your interactions with your child.

In the pedagogy of the oppressed, the oppressed often become oppressors. If you use cruelty to control your child, it is likely that she will use the same methods with her children and when you are old and frail, with you. Recognizing the ways in which you perpetuate small cruelties and putting a stop to them will improve your relationship with your child.

Creating a healthy mutuality with your child is necessary for her to be able to create mutuality with others. As a mother, I know that my commitment to doing what is in my boys' best interests enables them to recognize this quality or lack in others. As such, my children are able to spot authorities who do not have children's best interests at heart. They are also able to recognize the adults and children with whom they can build healthy relationships.

Since my children are only six and nine, I keep a pulse on them, continually asking them about their relationships with teachers and their friends at school. While it's their job to deal with friends, it's my responsibility to interact with adults. If an authority does or says something that doesn't feel right, my children tell me. Usually, a talk with this person will suffice. For instance, when my eldest son was five, he had a teacher who liked to read her students scary stories. He didn't tell me about this until one night, after I'd read him a bedtime story and told him it was time to go to sleep. He said, "Mom, I can't sleep because I have bad thoughts." When I asked him where these thoughts had come from, he told me that his teacher had read a story to the class about a man whose head had been cut off and rolled down the chimney into the fireplace. My son said that when he closed his eyes, he kept seeing the bloody head. I spoke with the teacher and she confirmed what my son had told me. When I suggested that the images from these stories were frightening to young children, she agreed to stop reading them.

Although sometimes you can make an impact on an authority, other times, there will not be much that you can do. For instance, my eldest son insists that one of his teachers doesn't like him. He says he is reprimanded for things that other kids do which go unpunished. Since it would be virtually impossible to prove that this teacher has a bias against him, I've used this as an opportunity to teach him how to deal with people who may not particularly like him. (Of course, we have also taken an honest look at his behavior and how he may be contributing to his teacher's view of him.) I've explained to him that throughout life, he will encounter those who play favorites or use their position to exercise prejudice. My son is learning to see that such a person's behavior reveals more about her than him. He's learning how to deal with someone who may not have *the* children's best interests in mind, yet succeed in spite of this. Such a situation presents a "teachable moment " and offers an opportunity for growth.

With regard to dealing with teachers and principals, make sure to pick your battles wisely. Don't go to the principal for every little thing. Take a stand when there's been a clear case of poor judgment or a violation of human rights. Be reasonable and respectful. Remember that, like you, authorities are learning how best to handle a variety of situations. Remember that a teacher must have control of the classroom and respect from students in order to do her job, so take care not to detract from her authority. Most teachers work hard and deserve our support and admiration.

With regard to your children's friends, know that your child will use his relationship with you as a blueprint for creating friendships with others. Teach your children, as I've taught mine, that friends are "people who bring out the best in them." Children who taunt them, hurt them or pressure them into doing things that conflict with their values are not among this group. Since your children will encounter such people throughout their lives, it's important to learn how to deal with them.

To teach your child how to recognize those who bring out the best in him, show him what that feels like. Every interaction with your child, especially those involving discipline, should be focused on inspiring his best.

The Dangers of Raising Children to Be Nice

Many parents make the mistake of raising children to be nice. What this means is that parents train children to please others and put others' needs before their own. In addition to creating an outward focus, the pressure to "be nice" often results in confusion over rules and values. For instance, it's common for parents to instruct their child to stay away from strangers, yet when their daughter meets a relative for the first time, the parents may order her to give that person a hug and kiss. If the child refuses or shies away, the parents may use guilt or shame to force compliance. By being more concerned about an adult's feelings of rejection than allowing their daughter to trust her instincts, the parents are putting the relative's needs above their child. It's sad when parents are more focused on what others think of them, rather than supporting the life-affirming instincts of their child.

The New Oxford American Dictionary defines the word *nice* as "pleasant or agreeable," but this is not its original meaning. The word "nice" originates from the Latin word *nescius* which means "ignorant" and comes from *nescire* "not know."

The implication is that in training your child to be nice, you raise her to ignore (be ignorant of) her instincts and naïve about other people's motives. (Refer to Chapter 5 and the discussion about human coyotes.) In a world in which children are regularly abducted from their homes, this puts a child at risk. Training a child to be nice divorces her from her instincts and powers of discernment, which are crucial self-preservation skills. A child who is taught to please others and disregard her feelings will attract those who intend to take advantage of her niceness.

Sociopaths are masters at using your niceness against you. Either they use *your* niceness to draw you into a trap or they use *their* niceness to trick you into believing that they are just like you. Ted Bundy, the serial killer, was a good example of a sociopath who perfected his niceness skills. In fact, most of those who knew him described him as a "nice guy" and were shocked to discover that he had committed multiple murders. In *The Gift of Fear*, Gavin de Becker warns: "We must learn and then teach our children that niceness does not equal goodness. Niceness is a decision, a strategy of social interaction; it is not a character trait. People seeking to control others almost always present the image of a nice person in the beginning. Like rapport building, charm, and the deceptive smile, unsolicited niceness often has a discoverable motive."

Raising children to be nice jeopardizes their safety. While they're figuring out how to please a stranger, they may be ignoring vital, instinctual signals. Such children are externally directed because they're more concerned with how others perceive them than how they feel inside. Such children do not have the security that comes from knowing who they are and trusting what they feel. Children disregard their needs and feelings because their parents have disregarded them.

Such children may grow into adults who are unable to create a healthy love relationship. Rather than lovers, they attract losers and users: the type of people who will drain them dry. Since they are used to pleasing others, they have no idea how to please themselves. In an effort to improve their relationships, they give more, hoping things will change, but they never do because the people they attract do not know how to act in the best interest of another human being. These children grow up to become adults who are the pleasers and the chronic hopers of society and spend their lives wallowing in despair. Girls are particularly prone to this, as they are more often raised to be nice, to take care of others' feelings, while ignoring their own, to be charming and pleasing to the eye.

When you raise a child to *act* in a certain way, rather than to *be* herself, you raise a child who is disconnected from her nature. Such a child will be confused about who she is, what she feels and what she wants from life. She'll look to others for direction and be easily swayed by their demands. If you raise your daughter to be "nice," she'll become a chameleon of sorts, changing her identity based on her perception of others' expectations. This makes for a desperately unhappy life.

Rather than raising your child to be "nice," raise her to be real. Encourage her to trust her instincts. If your child does not want to hug or kiss someone, don't force her. Don't sacrifice her in order to protect the feelings of an adult. Let your child select her friends, unless you feel strongly that a certain child is dangerous. Determine carefully what you define as dangerous and trust in your powers of discernment. Although you may consider a certain child a "bad influence," consider that this person can provide valuable opportunities for your child to learn to stand up to peer pressure and follow her inner compass. Sooner or later, your child will be forced to live and work with people who hold different values. Better she learn how to deal with such people now, while under your protective wing, then after she's gone off to college. By supporting your child and allowing her to make choices and mistakes, you encourage her to trust herself and find her way in the world.

Raise your child to trust her instincts and she will know and trust her feelings. This will allow her to choose friends who bring out the best in her. It will help her make value-laden choices in the face of peer pressure and behave in congruence with her beliefs. It will help her avoid people who *act* nice, but whose niceness is nothing more than a cleverly-crafted front. Your child will be able to sense situations that are dangerous and hone keen self-preservation skills that will prevent her from being tricked into the fold of a coyote who intends to use her and do her harm.

Rather than being other-directed, your child will follow her own internal compass. A child who is true to herself does not need to *act* "nice" or "good." Since this child has been treated respectfully by her parents, she naturally treats others with regard. Although she is kind, she is not a fool. She does not make the mistake of equating niceness with a requirement to sacrifice her needs or ignore her feelings in order to gain approval from others. This child pleases herself and in so doing, pleases those around her who have earned that right. Since this child lives her life from the inside out, she will choose a path that brings fulfillment and contributes to others. Since her feelings and intuitions have been supported since childhood, they will mature into accurate powers of discernment that will determine the people she invites into her life.

Some Decisions Last Forever

One of the highest realizations possible is to transcend the apparent dualities of life and come to the understanding that we are all connected because nothing is separate from God. This is the pinnacle of spiritual development. Although there have been a handful of children who came in with this realization (such as Jesus and Buddha), most of us move toward it by progressing through the stages of human development.

Humans are social animals whose evolution of identity progresses from the need to belong to a group, to the urge for individuation, contribution, self-actualization and finally, to the realization of our oneness. In this way, evolution is a spiral that returns us to our beginnings, but this time with awareness.

During your child's early years, his identity comes from a sense of place and purpose within the family. As he approaches school age, his identity expands to include relationships with peers and performance in school and extracurricular activities. The inherent danger of this time is that the child learns to measure himself by external gauges such as outside approval, rewards and grades. This is why I encourage you to follow the suggestions in Chapter 3 and give your child a spiritual name. In the face of all the pressures to conform and identify with the outside world, a spiritual name will help your child maintain an inner focus which is essential to his ability to thrive.

During the growing-up years, your child will learn about dualities: good and evil, empowerment and coercion, love and indifference, tolerance and prejudice, compassion and judgment, etc. Since these are the years of identity formation, when your child makes decisions that can last a lifetime, it is absolutely crucial that you know how he sees himself and how he views the world.

Because children are learning about opposites, they tend toward borderline thinking—seeing things in black and white. To illustrate, let me give you an example from my life. When my son was eight years old, he decided that he was "no good" in science on the basis of one test. These are the things you need to watch out for—the decisions your child makes, often during times of perceived failure, upset or crisis that are based on limited experience and can determine the direction of his life.

Helping Your Child Recognize the Snakes

During the school years, your child learns to socialize and develop relationships with his peers. The best guide for determining whether someone makes a good friend is to ask the question: "Does this person bring out the best in me?" If not, your child must reconsider the friendship.

Think about the qualities of a friend who brings out the best in you, so you can teach your child what to look for. A person who brings out the best in you has respect for your person, privacy and beliefs. Such a person will empower you with their support and care. Friends do not have a need to belittle you or make you feel bad about yourself or your choices. Friends inspire, rather than diminish you. They help you gain perspective. They keep your confidences and forgive you when you are grumpy because they know that sometimes, they get grumpy too.

Although your child's friends will not have all the qualities that a mature friend brings to a relationship, he should show the beginnings of them and with some consistency. If he does, he has a parent who has shown him respect and taught him how to cultivate healthy relationships.

There will be days when your child's friend sides against him or acts mean or cruel. All children struggle with a sense of loyalty and the surge of power that teasing brings. When your child is hurt or disappointed by a friend's behavior, explain that when his friend behaves like this, he is not acting like a friend. (Like the word "mother" and "father," "friend" should be used as a verb—a friend is "one who acts in the best interest of the relationship.") When this happens, I advise my children to be forthright and comment on the friend's behavior, saying something like: "Would you rather be mean or be my friend?" By doing this, your child gives the other child a choice. If the "friend" chooses to be cruel, then your child might come to realize that his "friend" has a limited capacity for friendship.

Throughout school, friendships come and go. A child who was once a good friend may decide when she hits adolescence that she wants to have friends who are more popular than your child. At this stage, children can be so cruel as to change friends, like they change their clothing. The loss of a confidante is as painful to a child as it is to an adult. The only difference is that an adult has more tools at her disposal to cope with it.

Keep a pulse on your child's friendships. Find out what's going on in her life. Find out how her friends are treating her and how their closeness has grown or receded over time. Share stories of your childhood friendships, rejections and your observations of how some people become more appearance-oriented during adolescence. Help your child to realize that the friends who choose her based on their desire to gain popularity are the social climbers who will use her as a ladder rung. Use the information in Chapter 6 to explain adolescent development and how some children reject their entire history to try on different hats. Whatever you do, reach out to your child. Don't leave her alone to sort out why a close friend has suddenly started treating her like dirt.

For younger kids, the lessons can be just as painful. Teach your children that like them, their friends are learning *how* to be good friends. Like them, their friends may occasionally make poor choices. At this stage, young children are resilient and quick to forgive, unless parents discourage them from doing so. Children's capacity for forgiveness allows them many opportunities to develop their sense of humanity and learn the basics of relationship.

A story that I touched on earlier will illustrate this point. When one of my children's friends was forced by his parents to apologize for stealing a game from us, I talked about the incident with my boys. We discussed how in choosing to take the game, the boy had valued a toy over his friendship with my son. Although he probably wasn't aware of it, this was the value behind his choice. When you are learning how to be a friend, it is tempting to put yourself above the friendship. Even as adults, we struggle with loyalty and feelings of self-entitlement.

When a friend betrays your child, underscore the values that were broken. In the case above, we talked about our belief that people matter more than things. Therefore, we do not steal from friends or others. Since children are learning how to make good choices, when someone has made an error, but takes the steps to make things right, their admission should be acknowledged and supported. Because the boy apologized, returned the game and learned from the incident, my boys quickly offered their forgiveness. Today, this boy remains a friend.

When your children are young, introduce the concept that through relationship, people reveal their values and beliefs about themselves. For instance, those who are dishonest with others are dishonest with themselves. You can only give others what you allow yourself. Understanding this helps children see the recursive nature of relationship, so they will be less likely to view others' weaknesses as a personal affront.

Since children are natural born students, they can easily see the difference between someone who is open to learning and someone who is not. When people make poor choices, they reveal their willingness to grow by admitting their errors and expending the energy to make things right. The child who is unwilling to make amends wants the benefit of a relationship without the work required of it. This child *needs* your child's friendship more than he *wants* it.

The distinction between *want* and *need* is crucial to understand. *Want* implies a choice and takes responsibility for it: I *want* to be with you and I am committed to giving my best to bring out the best in each of us. *Need* implies a lack and places responsibility for filling it squarely in someone else's lap: I *need* you to take care of me because I can't (or won't) take care of myself. Children need their parents, but healthy adult relationships are based on *wanting* to be together. The adult who *needs* a relationship is interested in meeting *his* needs. He's an unwilling partner in the dance of give-and-take that forms the foundation of relationship.

The only healthy relationship that is born on a one-way street is that of infant and mother. Of course, looking closer, you'll see that the intimacy of the birth experience: the blood, the struggling, the pushing, the mutual pain and later, the child's sweet suckling at the mother's breast creates an irrevocable bond that is immensely fulfilling and symbiotic. Remember that when a child is born, there are two births: the birth of the child and the birth of the mother.

Teach your child the difference between want and need and he'll know the secret of lasting friendship. Later, this will lead to the choice of a loving mate and the birth of children who will grow up knowing the secrets of relatedness. These children will go out into the world and seek their kind. In this way, a healthy relationship gives birth to itself again and again.

Dealing with Bullies

In the last section, we explored the idea that through relationship, others reveal their feelings about themselves. Knowing this makes it possible to see into the heart of the cruelest bully.

Those who harass, demean, taunt or physically assault others have no sense of inner joy. Although bullies seem powerful, they are driven by weakness. Rather than bring out the best in others, they bring out the worst. Usually, this is because they come from abusive, broken or neglectful homes in which they are bullied by siblings or parents.

In Chapter 4, I spoke of the distinction between the power of love and the love of power. The parents of bullies pass not their love, but their love of power to their child. Since children learn how to act by mimicking their parents, these children go to school and *re*-enact what they have experienced at home.

A father who works under the thumb of a ruthless boss and feels powerless to escape the drudgery of his life comes home and feels a sudden rush of power when he intimidates his son. Since he cannot derive this feeling elsewhere, he finds himself unable to stop, even

175

though he may see that he's damaging his son. The boy who is nothing more than a pawn in his father's quest for feeling powerful believes that this is how a real man acts. Since he dislikes feeling powerless, he assumes his father's persona and bullies others the way his father bullies him. Although the rush of power that he experiences is fleeting, it compels him because it gives him a much-needed feeling of control.

The key to stopping a bully in his tracks is to act in ways that would be impossible for him at home. To understand this, you have to realize that the bully has a script. All meanness and cruelty come from *re*-enacting this script. To interrupt it, you simply have to act in ways that halt his program. Understand that when you respond to a bully, you have a choice. Choose to act in ways that challenge his assumptions and you will catch the bully off-guard. He'll stammer, stumble and hesitate because someone has interrupted his movie about how things are supposed to go.

Although the action to take will vary with the bully, one thing that may work is to take a stand and make a loud demand for him to stop. This may stop the bully in his tracks because he can't make this same demand at home. It may cause the bully to look elsewhere for a victim. Obviously, this will not always work, but it's helpful to understand the way bullies think, so you can teach your children how to stop them.

When your child stands up to a bully, he may be showing him a way to inner power. By modeling behavior that is born of self-respect and saying, "Stop! I refuse to be treated like this," he may cause the bully to consider how he can stand up for himself at home. When the seemingly weak and small among us summon the courage to face the cruel forces of the world, they inspire us to grow.

Although standing up to a bully may not save your child from getting punched in the nose, it gives him a psychological edge that the bully doesn't have. In many ways, a bully is a caricature because his development has been stunted by his parent's use of force. He doesn't have the perspective, sense of self or security that a child gets from being loved. When a child who has self-respect stands up to another person's use of force, his integrity increases.

While understanding a bully's pain may not prevent your child's harassment, it helps put his behavior in perspective. Knowing that a bully is cruel because he feels powerless will help your child be less afraid of a person whose inner pain is obvious.

Although I do not advocate violence, I'm aware that many men, including my husband, would say that at some point, it's time to kick the bully's butt. While it may be appropriate to defend oneself, I don't think it's wise to retaliate. Force met with force doesn't solve the problem. In fact, it only worsens it, especially when dealing with someone who bullies others to overcome feelings of powerlessness. If your child humiliates a bully by beating him up in front of others, he may retaliate with a weapon much more dangerous than fists or tongue.

If a bully continually harasses your child, it's time for adults to intervene. Use good judgment here—don't turn every schoolyard conflict into an incident. If a child torments or harasses your child continually, document it. By putting each incident in writing, you're documenting your child's history of harassment by the bully. This will get the principal's attention. In such a case, the principal will act as a mediator between the two children and both sets of parents. If the bully has severe behavioral problems, then counseling will be recommended. Be advised that although a principal can recommend therapy, the parents have to bear the financial burden and recommendations may be ignored. If the parents are bullies themselves, they probably won't be interested in having a professional examine the roots of their child's behavior.

Teach your child to avoid conflict, whenever possible. Make sure he has close friends who can walk him to and from school and act as his witness on the playground. If your child is small and lacking in physical confidence, encourage him to get involved in a sport, such as martial arts which will teach him techniques of self-defense, along with principles of self-discipline and leadership.

Staying Actively Engaged in Your Child's Life

Many parents begin the journey of parenting by actively engaging every facet of their child's development and encouraging each small step. But as children grow and it takes more effort to find positive ways to relate to them, parental involvement wanes. By the time many kids are adolescents, they're doing life on their own with little or no parental guidance. Since this is a time when kids make decisions that can last a lifetime, parents must stay actively involved.

Studies have shown that as a child matures, the influence of peers surpasses the influence of parents and authorities. By contrast, there is only one study of which I'm aware that shows that this is not necessarily the case. Although I have done no research of my own, I wonder if the studies merely reflect a cultural tendency to support or withdraw from children during that oh-so-crucial stage of adolescence. When your child pushes you away, is often when she needs you most.

To ensure that you don't become estranged from your child, stay actively involved in her life. This means showing interest in what's going on in school, with friends, at home and with hobbies or sports. It means keeping a pulse on your child's emotional life: noticing if she exhibits sudden behavioral changes, if she changes friends or seems withdrawn or depressed. In Chapter 4, I talked about investing your child with interest. Genuine interest creates bonds that will sustain the parent-child relationship throughout adolescence and beyond.

If you start expressing your interest in the details of your child's life when she is young, this will create a lifelong habit of intimacy that will benefit you both. Although your child's willingness to offer details during the teenage years may diminish, she will still see you as a confidante for important issues. If you have taken the time to create a healthy relationship with your child, then she will use this model to cultivate a network of supportive friends. While you may not enjoy the frequency or deep connection that you had earlier, trust in the foundation that you have built. When your teenager needs you, she will ask for help. Be a silent witness, ready at a moment's notice to help sort out confusion or respond to emergency requests.

Since a discussion on parent-teenager relationships is another book, we will focus on ways to keep a pulse on your child, so a strong foundation will be laid before he reaches adolescence. Although I've talked about the importance of being involved in your child's life and showing genuine interest in his activities and fascinations, it bears repeating. I can't tell you how many times I have witnessed parents half-listening to their kids, or brushing them off when they're trying to share something that has captured their imaginations. This is when a rupture in the parent-child relationship begins. Tragically, it is initiated by the parents. When parents stop listening, kids stop too. Although I realize that some children talk in a continuous stream of consciousness, pick your moments wisely and listen actively to your kids. Doing so will make a difference in your relationship.

When watching your children perform in extracurricular activities, *watch* them. Don't view this as an opportunity to enjoy a social hour with other parents or read a magazine or book. I have been guilty of this. One day, my eldest son asked, "Mom, don't you come here to *watch* me?" I thought about it for a moment and realized that while it's okay to exchange greetings and comments with other parents, my heart and mind should be focused on my child. Watching him attentively shows my support and interest. Our bond grows through my child's subtle awareness that I am an active member of the audience. You may have heard of active listening—this is *active watching*.

Don't make the mistake of thinking that because your kids are older, they don't need you as their witness. At the martial arts studio where my children once took classes, there were always parents to watch the little kids' classes, but rarely were parents present to watch the teens. The parents dropped off their preteens and teenagers, viewing this as their time to do errands or stay in the car and read a book. While I understand that parents' lives are busy and filled with things to do and that they need personal time, make a commitment to watch your child's sport or activity at least once per week.

Watching your child play sports or engage in any hobby, regardless of whether he struggles or excels, is your way of participating in his growth. This is an opportunity that passes quickly. When you compare how your child is doing now to how he did last season, you will be astonished by his growth. For a child, there's no greater feeling than knowing that the people who love him most are in the stands, cheering him on when he succeeds and encouraging him when he stumbles.

Contrast this with children whose parents seldom or never watch them and therefore, have little idea of their burgeoning potential. My husband, Larry, was a pitcher who led his baseball team to win the College World Series in 1970. Throughout his little league, high school and college career, his parents never took enough of an interest in his athletic ability to watch him pitch a single game. Due to this, they had no idea of how good he was. They also had no idea *who* he was. To them, baseball was just a kid's game, like playing tag at the park. Finally, when my husband was twenty-two, his father traveled to the Series to watch him pitch. Even though my husband was an adult at the time, the poignancy of having his father present at the final game brought tears to his eyes.

Children love to be watched because they yearn to be *seen* and recognized for what they do and who they are. When a parent truly sees a child, the child feels loved and cherished. Know that in the future, your child will be there for you, as you have for him. Your presence is a present that will be returned to you one day.

Teaching the Value of Integrity

The famous psychiatrist Dr. Viktor Frankl once said, "Man is doomed to choice." When faced with tough choices, some people act in congruence with their values, some do what they think they can get away with, while others do nothing at all. Those who fail to act turn away from choice, "letting the chips fall where they may." By failing to choose, they have made a choice.

This is why in Chapter 1, I asked you to clearly define a vision for your child. Your vision is a distillation of your deepest beliefs and heartfelt yearnings for your child. It is a conscious commitment that will guide your choices as a parent. To make the right decision in any situation, use your vision to discover what will serve your child's best interest. "Best interest" does not mean overindulgence. The idea is to help your child step toward the kind of human being you want him to become. If your vision fails to guide the evolution of his humanity, rethink it. Even if your child doesn't seem to move in this direction, don't give up on him. If you let the chips fall where they may, they will fall at your feet and your family will trip over the mess you have made by living a life undirected by vision.

By making conscious choices, you teach your child to do the same. This lays the foundation for making the tough choices that build character and self-discipline. Although teaching your child to make hard choices should be done from an early age, it is never too late to start. We all yearn to feel good about our choices.

As discussed previously, human existence is replete with dualities.

Good vs. evil, care vs. indifference, tolerance vs. prejudice, power of love vs. love of power, etc. Helping your child struggle to find a balance between the dualities of life will help him create his own internal value system that is born of insight and reflection. By discussing the spectrum of human consciousness and showing your child how to weigh the scales in favor of that which is life-affirming, your child will come to know himself and how he feels about important issues. As such, his choices will reveal a contemplative mind, a respectful nature, a humane heart, strength of character and integrity. This is how a child develops true self-esteem: by acting in congruence with deeply examined and cherished values. Integrity is the true indicator of self-worth.

As such, while your child is learning to make tough choices, reserve harsh judgment. It is the still, small voice within that is the arbiter of such choices and is experienced as the voice of conscience. If you judge a child who is learning *how* to make hard choices, then your harsh voice will become his inner critic which drowns out the voice within that knows the difference between a choice that brings out the best in him and one that doesn't.

When a child fails to make the best choice, approach her with compassion. Talk about the choice she made and ask how she arrived at it. Ask her how she feels about the choice and how she thinks it has impacted her and others. Ask her what she has learned and if she would make that choice again. Ask her if she was aware that she had other choices at the time. Would another choice have been better? How? Help her to recognize that the voice that offers the best direction is often quiet and non-insistent. It says what it has to say, but doesn't threaten, bribe or force. It speaks the truth and then falls silent. It is the voice that knows how choices can be made for the benefit of all. In order to hear it, your child simply needs to listen and learn to distinguish it from the myriad of voices that exhibit their self-interest. Be patient: learning how to make better choices is a function of brain development. (This is an important issue for adolescents. During the teenage years, the prefrontal cortex is shaped and pruned. This affects a teen's ability to curb impulses, set priorities, organize thought processes and consider consequences. As I've mentioned before, when your teen is pushing you away is when she needs you most.)

Discuss how choices that conflict with inner values create a nagging sense of "*dis*-ease" and chip away at feelings of self-worth. These choices lead to more of the same and create habitual behaviors. Poor choices weaken us. Choices that reflect our values increase integrity and assist us in making better choices next time. Such choices make us strong.

In Chapter 5, I encouraged you to define a Family Code of Honor. If you have not yet done so, please talk about basic values with your children and create an agreed-upon family code. Include the virtue of integrity as a way of being that honors the entire contract. By engaging your child with each tenet of the code, you give him a model for creating and adhering to his own self-created code during the turbulent times of adolescence. When it seems as though his world is crashing down around him, your child will use his code to forge a path through the debris. This won't be *your* code or the code of some institution or organization. It will be *his* code—a set of virtues that may be based on yours, but belong to him because he has earned the right to claim them for his own. This is integrity—the greatest security humans have.

Teaching Your Child to be Self-sufficient

Although childhood is a time of play and discovery, children should be given responsibilities that progressively teach them to be self-sufficient. Parents who do everything for their children are at risk of becoming martyrs. This helps no one and does children a great disservice because it raises them into adults who don't know how to care for themselves or be of service to others.

Assigning chores is an effective way to help children develop a growing sense of independence. Chores should be age-appropriate and designed to foster a sense of competence and shared responsibility. Children need and want to help. Being a contributing member of the family gives them a sense of place and purpose and teaches that we must share our strengths with others.

Children five years old and younger should be given simple tasks, such as helping to clean their rooms and other messes. At this stage of development, chores should be cooperative, meaning that a child assists a parent and learns how to approach, tackle and complete a task.

From ages six to ten, children can be expected to do some chores independently, primarily the chores that they helped out with previously. For instance, while you can expect your kids to straighten up their rooms, don't expect them to do a major re-organization. If a sorting project is well overdue, help your children go through their bureau, closet and toy box. In my family, we do this twice per year. We throw away things that are broken and donate or sell at a neighborhood garage sale those things that the children have outgrown or no longer want or use.

Between the ages of six through ten, children can carry their dirty dishes to the counter, rinse them off and load the dishwasher. They can vacuum common areas, straighten their bed covers and take their laundry to the laundry room. They can also help with seasonal chores, such as shoveling the walkway after a light snow. Parents can have their children make school lunches, but check to make sure that they're packing them with nutritious food. A good way to ensure this is to fill your pantry with fresh produce and healthy snacks.

Children older than ten can wash and/or fold their laundry. This skill becomes especially helpful during the teenage years, when some kids change their clothing several times per day. At this age, they can learn to cook and help prepare the family meals or clean up the kitchen.

Although I've given you some basic recommendations, chores will vary based upon your lifestyle and your children's level of maturity. In delegating chores, keep several keys in mind. Chores should be designed to help your child help himself and generate a burgeoning sense of self-sufficiency. Doing chores should be seen as a child's way of making a contribution to the family. Although helping out is good for children, some parents see their kids as a free labor force. To avoid this mindset, design tasks that are age-appropriate and serve the best interests of your child by helping him become progressively independent.

Teach your children to work cooperatively on a single task. For instance, if two children share a room, they should clean it up together, with the older child handling the more complex tasks. This is good for the eldest child because it challenges his abilities, but it's also good for the younger one because it gives him something to aspire to. When he gets older, he will be able to handle the bigger jobs, like older brother.

Previously, I wrote about the value of responsiveness. Teach your children to be responsive by encouraging everyone to pitch in and help with accidental spills or unexpected messes. This avoids the practice of assigning blame and generates a climate of helpfulness. A sense of responsiveness impels children to take responsibility for the environment, rather than their small corner of the world. It is the attitude that one does what is necessary, rather than refusing to help because it's "not my job."

When you witness your children being responsive on their own, you will realize what a beautiful way this is to show their care for others. The other day, while I was cooking dinner, my eldest son reached into an open cereal box and accidentally knocked it to the floor. Cereal flew everywhere. Immediately, my youngest son grabbed the broom and together they cleaned up the spill. I didn't say a word— I didn't have to. Had they happened to look up at me, they would have seen the tears welling in my eyes.

Although this is not a book on raising teenagers, for the benefit of parents whose children are on the cusp of adolescence, I'll continue, so you can start to think about which chores will prepare your teen for adulthood.

The teenage years are the last years that a parent has to prepare a child for life as an adult. The key is to focus on preparation. Soon, your child will be venturing out on her own, so teaching a teenager to be self-sufficient is paramount. If she does not know how to cook meals, do laundry and take care of a car, you will set her up for frustration, overwhelm and failure. Rather than relying on herself, she will be forced to rely on others.

During the teenage years, a child's chores around the house should increase to include doing her own laundry, helping out with cooking, yard work and cleaning. Although your child may grumble about this, remind her that you're preparing her to be a self-sufficient adult.

If your child has a car, responsibilities should include checking the gauges, tire pressure, filling the gas tank, learning how to check fluid levels and change the oil. If your child does not have her own car, but drives yours, the responsibilities should be the same. Teenagers should be taught how to jump-start a battery and how to move a car out of the flow of traffic should it stall. They need to know how to operate a jack and change a tire.

Teens should be taught the basics of car operation, so if trouble occurs, they'll know what to do. Parents should advise their children to fill up the gas tank when the gauge is at the halfway mark, so they won't risk running out of gas. A simple reminder which a parent directs to herself aloud, while driving with her children, "Oh, the tank is half full … time to fill it up," will become internalized by the teen. In order to get your child into the habit, adopt it first yourself.

Teenagers should be advised about the risks of picking up hitch-hikers and/or hitchhiking if they have car trouble. Extra money or "funny money" should be hidden in a special place in the car that is reserved for use during emergencies.

Don't assume that your child has been taught in school what he needs to know about defensive driving. When he gets his learner's per-mit, take him on the road as much as possible. The more experience and guidance he has in all kinds of weather and road conditions, the more likely he is to develop the judgment that will assist him in mak-ing split second decisions that could prevent an accident and save his life. Although there are software packages available that simulate a variety of driving situations, experience is the best teacher.

Know that your child will be faced with decisions regarding dri-ving and drugs. Teach kids to think about the consequences of driving drunk or of putting their lives in the hands of a friend who has been drinking.

When I was in high school, one of my male friends went to a party with another friend and they both got drunk. After the party, my friend staggered to his car to drive himself and his buddy home. On the way, he crashed the car. He survived with major injuries, but the other boy died. For a long time, he wished that he had died. The teenager who was killed that day was considered a "golden boy"—an incredibly handsome, athletic, intelligent, popular kid—who was loved by all. We mourned his loss and with it, the loss of our sense of invul-nerability. Thinking about him now, I wonder what kind of man he would have become. I wonder what contributions he might have made if only he had made a better choice.

Before your kids are of driving age, share personal stories from your life about the dangers of driving to give your teen perspective. According to statistics, twice as many teen drivers die in car accidents than adults. Although the last thing you want to do is frighten your kids, most teens have a strong sense of invincibility and the unrealistic conviction that "that will never happen to me." This is particularly important in terms of teaching teenagers about driving and drugs. One moment could forever change their lives. Assure your child that if he's ever in a situation in which it seems that the only option is to ride home with an intoxicated friend, he has a better choice: to call you, so you can come and get him.

Share your personal stories and read stories from the newspaper that show that drunk driving accidents happen to teens. The idea is to increase awareness and encourage teens to think about to whom they entrust their lives.

Teenagers who have a firm sense of purpose about their lives, who know their values and are not easily swayed by others, realize that choices have consequences and are able to stand up to peers and turn down drugs. It's not as simple as Nancy Reagan's slogan "Just say, 'No.'" Whoever came up with this didn't understand what causes people to turn to drugs in the first place.

Children should be taught the basics of emergency healthcare. For instance, knowing how to perform CPR and the Heimlich maneuver are important aspects of emergency care that everyone can learn. Many years ago, when my sister was at a Dodger game with her boyfriend, he was eating peanuts by tossing them high in the air and catching them in his mouth. When a peanut lodged in his esophagus and he couldn't breathe or speak, he saved his own life by ramming his abdomen against the back of a stadium chair, until he expelled the peanut. Had he relied on my sister to save him, he would have died because she didn't know how to perform the maneuver at the time.

Teaching Your Child How Money Works

Several years ago, I spoke to an elderly woman who admitted to me that soon after she was newly married, her husband had almost divorced her on the spot when the police informed him that she had written a series of bad checks. After he calmed down, he discovered that she hadn't done this intentionally—she didn't understand how checking accounts worked. As a teenager, she had watched her mother write checks for this and that, but had never seen her make a deposit because her father made them on the way home from work. As a girl, growing up in the 1930's, her parents had not taught her anything about money, except how to spend it. As a result, her concept of checking accounts was based on a magical view of the world: to her, checking accounts were like money trees. When her husband realized this, he had a good chuckle and explained the ins and outs of checking accounts.

Although this woman's naivete seems implausible, her husband confirmed the story. Young children who have magical ideas about life hold on to these ideas, until experience proves them false. If an experience is not forthcoming, these misperceptions are carried into adulthood. Since you don't want your grown child to get into trouble for mismanaging money, teach her how money works.

Many parents do this by starting a savings account for their child. Several years ago, when I started my children's savings accounts, they were thrilled to have money of their own. When they receive money as a gift for holidays or birthdays, they are required to invest a percentage in their savings and can spend the rest. This experience has taught them how to save for the future, how compounding interest works and how to weigh the value of purchasing one item over another.

When children grow older, teach them about the stock market and real estate. If you don't know much about it, learn together. If you don't have money to risk, use "play" money. Teaching your kids how to generate passive income helps them learn how to make money work for them which is different than working for money. For more on this, see the Resources section of my web site.

One way to teach children how to manage money is to give them an allowance. Our children receive two dollars per week, so they can buy small items, save for more expensive things like collectible cards and learn how to spend their money wisely. This allowance is not for the chores they do around the house. In our family, we emphasize the value of responsiveness—the idea that it is everyone's responsibility to pitch in and help. We do our chores because we care about each other and because we like living in a home that is reasonably clean and well-maintained. Everyone in our family has jobs to do and the children are no exception. Occasionally, though, we offer to pay them a certain amount to do extra chores, like sweeping the deck or cleaning the track in the sliding glass door.

Although some parents give money for good report cards, I don't advocate this because I think that school performance should be motivated by a desire to learn, rather than monetary reward. As mentioned in Chapter 4, studies have shown that rewards extinguish internal motivation. When you reward a child for learning, you may be dousing his inner flame.

For the same reason, I believe that children should not be paid for good behavior. I know a boy whose allowance is based on this. He gets one dollar per day for "being good." Again, I think this is dangerous. A child's behavior should be motivated not by money, but by humane values and the desire to share his strengths with others.

Answer your children's questions with regard to money. My children have already asked how much we spend on our home and cars. I've explained to them how bank loans work. Since they have an idea of how much things cost, they appreciate when we can afford to buy them extras.

When your children become teenagers, help them start a checking account. Although your name will probably have to be on the account until they turn eighteen, treat the account as though it belongs solely to your child. To begin, transfer some money from their savings into their checking account. If they get a summer job, they will be able to deposit and/or cash their paychecks. When they make purchases, they can pay by check, so they'll learn about bank fees and account balancing. If they're in high school and have a job, you may want to co-sign on a credit card, so they can learn about making small purchases on credit. Teach them how interest works, so they'll understand that getting an item on sale is costing them more if they charge it and pay it off over time. Illustrate how this works with concrete examples and comparisons. Make them aware of the high interest charged by department store credit cards.

Teach your child how to work and save for things he can't afford. For instance, if your preteen wants a car, tell him that he must save and contribute to the cost. He can get a job on weekends or during the summer or do odd jobs around the neighborhood.

Another option is to make a loan. When I was sixteen, I asked my grandmother to lend me $1500 for my first car. Businesswoman that she was, she made me sign a contract, stating that I would repay the full amount of the loan including interest. She charged me ten percent, the same interest rate that the banks charged at the time. Every month, I made a payment. I paid for gas and insurance too. When I had paid off the loan, I understood how loans worked. My grandmother, whose grown children constantly borrowed but seldom repaid her, bragged that she would loan money to her sixteen-year-old granddaughter any time.

A few years later, I decided to buy a newer car and this time, my boyfriend's stepfather co-signed on a bank loan. Since he knew that I had repaid my debt to my grandmother, he was confident that I would be responsible for the loan.

Teaching Children How to Live with Death

In our culture, we don't talk about death until after someone has died. Even then, some families refuse to talk about it. Rather than being straightforward, people use euphemisms like *he passed on, we lost him* or *he's in heaven*. This creates questions in a child's mind that lead him to believe that those who have died may physically return. If a person has passed, where did he go? If he's lost, shouldn't we try to find him? If he's in heaven, can we visit? Using euphemisms to skirt the truth makes children think that death is unnatural. If death is unnatural, then it's natural to fear it.

Death is permanent—at least for the living—the loved one does not come back in the form that we have known and cherished. Life and death go hand in hand. What is born must die. These are indisputable facts of our existence.

The antidote for a fear of death is living fully. When you live your life with intention, purpose, compassion and integrity, you live without fear of death because you know who you really are. Those who are afraid to die are afraid of life. The famous therapist Fritz Perls once said that fear is "excitement without a breath." If people can turn their fear of death into the excitement of discovering who they are, they will die with a smile on their face, knowing that they have *lived*. Although death may seem scary, it is really just a surrender to something greater than "the known."

The concept of death is simple, but we complicate it with fear. The reason that we have such difficulty accepting it, unlike some cultures, is that we do not have ceremonies that acknowledge death as part of life. Children and families need to participate in rituals that recognize death as life's companion. In *Good Grief: Helping Groups of Children When a Friend Dies*, author Sandra Fox says that children need to know three things about physical death. Death means that your body totally stops working. Death is irreversible. Death happens to everyone.

The permanence of physical death may be shocking to a child, but accepting it helps him move forward through the grief process, rather than clinging to the hope that the dead person will return.

One of the worst things that can happen to a child is the unexpected death of a loved one. If the child has been prepared for death and it has been talked about in the home, then there is a foundation for understanding.

When I was twelve years old, my Uncle Roger died. Of all the people in my life, he was the one person with whom I most connected. I looked up to him and thought that he was "cool." We used to go for drives in his purple, flower-covered dune buggy or his white Chevy van. He was kind to me; he asked me questions and listened intently to my answers as though I had something interesting to say. I loved him deeply and anticipated our time together. Then one day, he was gone. To me, it was as though he'd vanished. No one talked about his death. I wasn't taken to his funeral. My parents told me that Roger was in heaven. My father was so grief-stricken that I don't think he had the heart to help me with my loss.

Looking back, I realize that if someone had first laid the groundwork and taught me about death's universality and permanence, I would have appreciated my uncle more while he was alive. I would have told him how much I enjoyed his company and how grateful I was to have him in my life. I thought these things, but doubt I said them. Knowing the finality of death would have prevented me from fantasizing the possibility of his return. While I knew that people died,

I never imagined in my wildest dreams that it could happen to my strong, vibrant, twenty-something-year-old uncle.

Twenty years later, when I learned about the Mexican-Indian celebration, "El Dia del Muerte" or "The Day of the Dead," I realized instantly its personal and cultural significance. Rather than denying death, Mexican-Indian people celebrate it, welcome it as friend and teacher and honor those it has taken.

"The Day of the Dead" is based on the Native American Indian belief that life and death are intertwined. Both are part of the Circle. When we die, we return to the place from which we came.

Native Americans advise you to "remember your death," while you're alive. When you live your life with the realization that tomorrow may never come, you awaken to life's sacredness and trivialities fall away. When death is part of your consciousness, you summon the courage to step toward the realization of your dreams. Each moment becomes one of conscious, loving intention. When you live this way, any day can be what Native American warriors called, "A good day to die." Only one who has achieved a sense of purpose and imperturbability can make such a proclamation.

Due to my experience with my uncle, I feel strongly that parents should talk to children about death before it happens to someone in their lives because it *will* happen. Since my children were old enough to talk, I've used Nature's cycles to discuss the physical reality of death. As winter draws near, we notice how bugs die, animals hibernate and plants go dormant. We talk about how the fly trapped in the spider's web becomes nourishment and how the leaves of the deciduous trees burst forth in one final flash of color, before they scatter to become a winter blanket for the ground. The reality of death reveals the nature of the Circle.

Recently, while attending a seminar on grieving, a minister in the audience raised his hand. He said that the children in his area who grow up on ranches and farms seem to accept death more readily than other kids. Living close to nature provides ample opportunities for children to observe that life and death go hand in hand.

Of course, talking about death with kids brings up tough questions. In my family, such talks have made my children aware that I will die. When these fears arise, I ask them to feel in their hearts how tenderly I love them. The love they feel creates a *presence* which is with them whether I am or not. Although a mother carries a fetus inside her womb for nine months, a child carries his mother's heart within him forever.

No matter what happens, my children know that I am with them because I have seen into their hearts. In this way, I teach my children that while the body dies, love endures. This quells their fears because they know that what they need most from me—the feeling of being seen, accepted and cherished for who they are—has become a fixture of their sense of self. This gives rise to an essential truth: love transcends the physical and the limits of space and time.

Of course, I also tell my children that I am healthy and that I intend to live to see them grow into adults. As proof of my intention, I eat well, get enough sleep, play and exercise. I take vitamins and buckle up before we drive somewhere in the car. Such actions illustrate that there are concrete measures that people can take to maintain health and increase safety.

Some people might be disturbed by the thought of teaching children about death before it touches someone close to them. To them, I pose the question—which is more resourceful—to prepare your children for death's eventuality or deny that it exists until you are proven wrong? Talking about death with sensitivity doesn't make a child fearful; refusing to discuss it does.

The Mother of Us All

Native Americans see the Earth as mother. Since my children were old enough to engage in conversation, I have told them that they have two mothers. If you ask my six-year-old who his mother is, he'll answer with a question, "Which one? I have two: my mommy and Mother Earth." Although this is a Native American belief, it is a spiritual one. Remember that while religion divides us into separate camps, spirituality unites us on common ground. Nothing is more common than the Earth.

Mother Earth is the cradle from which we are born and the final resting place for our bodies. In the Native American world, since "mother" is a verb, teach your child that the earth reveals herself as mother by acting as his caretaker: by providing food, water, shelter, air and all the elements that sustain human life. Mother Earth is the solid ground that we stand upon, yet she yields to the construction of our homes, roads, buildings, tunnels, subways and bridges. Even though she travels around the sun at almost 67,000 miles per hour, her gravity holds us close, the way a mother cradles a baby to her breast.

Recognizing Earth as mother, gives your children a sense of security because no matter where they are, one of their mothers is present. They simply need to look around or shift their awareness to the soles of their feet. This feeling of relatedness to Mother Earth will deepen into a sense of relatedness to life in all its teeming variations. Whatever your beliefs, whatever the color of your skin, you depend on Mother Earth. As your children grow, they will become caretakers of that which has been their guardian and share this with their children. This is how love and awareness of the sacred grows.

Awakening from the Dream

In the Native American world, it is believed that when we live, we dream and when we die, we awaken from the dream. (Other indigenous people, including the Irish, believed this too which is why they hold "a wake" for the dead.) In fact, this is the meaning of the dream catcher—a circular symbol with a beaded, hand-woven center often sold in Native American gift stores and recently popularized by mainstream culture. Contrary to how Stephen King portrayed this sacred symbol in a recent movie, the function of the dream catcher is not to ward off evil spirits, but to remind us that we are here to live our dreams.

Native Americans believed that life is an illusion or *maya,* which originates from the Sanskrit *ma* and means "create." Life, then, is about making your dreams come true or as I like to put it: *dreaming yourself awake.*

You dream yourself awake as you unfold your nature and realize your purpose here on Earth. Purpose has little to do with money or will or ego—it is a gift of Nature—the work that the Creator placed in your heart and the reason that you were born into this world. Although discovering your purpose may not necessarily bring what mainstream culture deems success, it will create fulfillment and a world enlivened with the vibrancy of love, meaning and relatedness.

Purpose unfolds from strength. Strength is revealed by nature. Through knowledge of your nature and contribution of your strengths, you give birth to the spiritual self and slowly awaken from the dream. When this happens, the ego self yields to the greater Self that has been quietly guiding you all along.

As a parent, it is your honor to polish the "turquoise in the rough" that is your child. Like Kevote in *Spirit-Boy and the Gift of Turquoise*, when you polish your child's heart with love, respect and wonder, his nature will be revealed.

Each piece of turquoise has its own individual matrix. In Spirit Boy's case, it took the form of a lightning bolt. When lightning strikes the atmosphere, it bonds nitrogen to oxygen, creating a compound that is essential to healthy plant life. Although it may be hard to believe that lightning is a key to Earth's abundance, each day, it strikes the planet over eight million times somewhere along its surface. In much the same way, nature is the key to our abundance. Each of us has something unique to offer to the whole. When we express what is in our nature, others profit and we enrich our capacity for joy. As Kevote discovered in *Spirit-Boy and the Gift of Turquoise*, by helping your child unfold his uniqueness, you plumb the wellspring of your heart. The evolution of the parent-child relationship is a gift for child and parent.

A child who is raised with a vision that is designed to stir him from the dream will lead a life of contribution because his actions will naturally unfold from his desire to fully know his heart. In his humble quest to know himself, he will reach beyond his ego and come to know the hearts of others. In such a world, a love of nature empowers all.

By setting your child on nature's path, you give him a compass to the Self. In this act, is the key to his transcendence. As spiritual beings living on a physical plane, it is our destiny to awaken from the dream while living on the Earth.

Conclusion

In this book, I've hoped to illustrate the mutuality of the parent-child relationship. Parenting is as much about your child's development, as it is about your own. As you raise your child with vision and knowledge of his nature, you touch his essence and the core of who you are. As you do what's necessary to raise a humane being, you become one. Every interaction with your child affords you the opportunity to inspire your child and aspire to the highest in yourself. In this way, your child becomes the muse to the sage in you and you become the leaping-off point for your child.

Throughout this book, I've woven together two seemingly disparate ideas—Native American philosophy and developmental psychology—to create a way of parenting that is grounded in the natural world, yet spiritually based. Although at first glance Native American philosophy may seem removed from psychology, Native Americans were the first psychologists because they understood that knowing nature is the path to understanding self and others.

Native American philosophy is an invaluable tool in creating strong parent-child bonds because it's based on stewardship and evolution of consciousness. The bonds you create with your child form a circle of love that grows as he creates relationships with others. As the circle expands, a parent becomes a parent of *the* children and a child becomes a citizen of the world. As parents and children become caretakers of one another and of Mother Earth, more people will come to realize that we are all related because we stand on common ground. This is the scope of parenting to which I invite you to aspire.

In this book, you have been given valuable tools for establishing and maintaining a healthy parent-child bond. You began this journey by reading *Spirit-Boy and the Gift of Turquoise* and asking yourself what kind of story you have been creating for your child. By operating from vision rather than fear, you have made a conscious commitment to guide the unfolding of your child's spiritual sense of self.

In Chapter 3, you learned as Kevote did in *Spirit-Boy and the Gift of Turquoise* that when you polish your child's uniqueness and encourage it to shine, you see into his heart. In this way, a child learns how to *keep* his nature, hone his strengths and use them in service of the people. By giving your child a spiritual name, you ground him in the natural world and set him on the path of fullness. Such a child will lead an extraordinary life.

Chapter 4 revealed that true discipline empowers your child to develop the self-discipline to walk the path toward his dreams. You learned the difference between the power of love and the love of power and that to teach self-discipline, you must be willing to look yourself squarely in the eye.

In Chapter 5, you learned that by creating a family code, you give your child the tools to formulate his own code and follow it, despite peer pressure, opportunity or crisis. You learned that it is crucial to teach children conflict resolution skills, so they will practice diplomacy as adults.

In Chapter 6, our exploration of human development created a map that helped you develop reasonable expectations for your child's behavior. It also helped you see where you stand along the path of maturation of consciousness. Your realization of where you are on the path of human development and what you need to do to grow sets a precedent for personal growth that will be adopted by your child. The mutuality of this interplay is stunning.

By knowing your child's nature and giving him the tools he needs to thrive, you have set him squarely upon the path of self-actualization. Although initially it may have seemed that parenting asked much of you, you have come to see (as Kevote did in *Spirit-Boy and the Gift of Turquoise*) that ultimately, parenting is a gift you give yourself. By bringing out the best in your child, you *become* the highest in yourself.

In order to raise children to lead purposeful lives and aspire to greater evolution of consciousness, we must turn back to the world that our ancestors turned away from. This doesn't require that we deny the comforts of modern life—it means that we must bridge the gap between the world we envision and the one in which we live.

The time is ripe. The children await you.

Afterword

If this book has inspired you, please recommend it to your friends, family, colleagues and acquaintances. With your help, we can work toward a shared vision that encourages the parents of the world to help their children make the leap toward living lives of compassion, consciousness, purpose and fulfillment.

Additional copies of this book may be purchased from my web site www.parenting-child-development.com or by mailing in the Order Form on the last page of this book.

In January of 2005, I will begin publishing a quarterly email newsletter called, "The Circle," which will further elaborate the tenets of this book. If you are interested in subscribing, please send in the Order Form.

As a valued reader, I invite you to send me your comments or opinion of this book. Please understand that by doing so, you give me permission to post your comments, name and state on my web site and/or in promotional materials. Although I ask you to include your contact information, it will not be shared with other companies. Please understand that although I can't respond to individual questions, your concerns will be counted and considered and may be used to develop future material that is of interest to other parents. I want to help you help your children. I want you to feel fulfilled as a parent. To show my appreciation for your willingness to share what's in your heart, I have included a little gift—my husband's *Prayer to Consciousness*—a prayer that my family uses to evoke a sense of wonder, wisdom and appreciation.

Please take the survey on the next page to tell me what you most yearn for as a parent and how I can better serve you and your family in the future. (*Keepers of the Children* is the first in a trilogy of parenting books.) Send your completed survey to:

Walk in Peace Productions
POB 12396
Reno, NV 89510-2396
Attention: Reader Feedback and Review

Survey for "Keepers of the Children"

(If you have borrowed this book from a friend or library, please fill out the survey on my web site, rather than writing in the book. Go to: www.parenting-child-development.com/parent-survey.html.)

Name:

Address:

City, State, Zip:

Gender: [ ] Female   [ ] Male

Age:

Country of Birth:

Ethnicity:

Highest Education Level Achieved:

Is your family a mixed race family? If so, which races?

Number and ages of children in your home:

What you liked best about this book:

What you learned in this book and would like to know more about:

What you hoped to learn, but found missing in this book:

Any concepts presented in this book that you found confusing and for which you'd like clarification:

Your greatest concern for your children's future:

Your greatest concern for the future of the children of the world:

Your deepest wish for your children:

Your biggest fear or worry about your parenting skills:

What do you most need to feel fulfilled as a parent:

Future subjects you'd like to explore:

Would a parenting seminar based on the concepts in this book be helpful to you? If a seminar were offered in your area, would you attend?

Would you be interested in a teleseminar—a seminar conducted by phone?

Comments or suggestions:

Bibliography

Buber, Martin, *I and Thou Dialogue.* Simon & Schuster, New York, 1978.

Covey, Stephen, *Seven Habits for Highly Effective Families.* Golden Books, New York, 1997.

DeBecker, Gavin, *The Gift of Fear.* Little, Brown & Company, Boston, 1997.

Erdoes, Richard & Ortiz, Alfonso, *American Indian Myths and Legends.* Pantheon Books, New York, 1984.

Erikson, Erik, *The Life Cycle Completed.* W.W. Norton & Company, New York, 1982.

Erikson, Joan, *Wisdom and the Senses.* W.W.Norton & Company, New York, 1988.

Frankl, Viktor E., *Man's Search for Ultimate Meaning.* MJF Books, New York, 2000.

Fox, Sandra, *Good Grief: Helping Groups of Children When a Friend Dies.* New England Association for the Education of Young People, Boston, 1988.

Harris, Bill. *Thresholds of the Mind.* Centerpointe Press, Oregon, 2002.

Kohn, Alfie. *Punished by Rewards.* Houghton Mifflin Company, New York, 1983.

Hawkins, David R., M.D., Ph.D., *Power vs. Force: The Hidden Determinants of Human Behavior*, Hay House, Inc., 2002.

Psychology Today, January/Feb 116. Jean King Ph.D. Sussex Publishers, New York, 1996.

Pearce, Joseph Chilton, *The Biology of Transcendence.* Park Street Press, Vermont, 2002.

Peck, M. Scott, *People of the Lie,* Touchstone Books, New York, 1998.

Tzu, Sun *The Art of War,* Dover Publications, New York, 2002.

Williams, Arlene, *Tales from the Dragon Cave,* Waking Light Press, 1995.

Prayer for a Conscious Life

by Larry Ramirez
(Pascua Yaqui and Chirricahua Native American Indian)

Oh, Great Spirit whose voice I hear in the wind and whose breath gives life to all the world, hear me. I need your strength and I need your wisdom.

Let me walk in beauty and make my eyes behold the red and purple wonderment of your sunsets. Let me know the meaning of the seasons of life. Let me smile and always be in awe of how things change. Let this wonderment open my heart and mind to all, so I can feel and see the balance you have given me.

Help me to understand humanity. Let me never forget that human beings are the humblest of all creatures for we are born without direction. Help me to remember that even though we come in many shapes and colors, there is only one race—the human race.

Help me to create ceremony in life and remember that we are spiritual beings in human form. Let my experiences elevate my spiritual nature and help me to evolve.

Make my hands respect the things you have made. Make my ears open to your voice. Let my eyes see what is real in the balance of life. Make me wise so I may understand the things you have taught my people. Help me to feel your spirit when I am lost. Help me to see where I can have impact that heals. Let me learn the lessons that you have hidden in every leaf and rock. Let me learn from my joy and from my pain.

Creator, let me know my nature so I can find like kind and be part of the balance of life. I strive to be my nature which you have put inside me, like a seed in soil. Let life nurture me and if not, allow me to see the truth, so I can find a place to grow and prosper. Then I can know true love, family, balance and meaning. Then I will be free and have respect for all creatures.

Oh, Great Spirit, I seek you not to be greater than my brothers and sisters, but to understand the lessons I need to learn to fight my greatest enemy—inhumanity in myself and others.

Make me always ready to come to you with clean hands and straight eyes, so when life fades and I return to the Spirit World, I will become part of the light. As day passes to night, so does the mystery of life continue to the Great Mystery of the universe and beyond.

Let my children's children's children say this world is a better place for me having been here. Teach me to walk in peace and give respect to all my relations—for we are all related.

Resources

The Heart Math Institute:

www.heartmath.org

Information on recommended meditation CD or tape:

www.parenting-child-development.com/meditation-lessons.html

Animal Spirit Necklaces:

www.parenting-child-development.com/resources.html

 Dream Catchers:

www.parenting-child-development.com/resources.html

Teaching children how money works:

www.parenting-child-development.com/resources.html

About the Author:

Laura Ramirez lives in the sage-dotted foothills of Nevada with her husband Larry, a Pascua-Yaqui Native American Indian, and her two sons, Dakotah and Colt. Laura has been publishing *Family Matters Online Parenting Magazine* for the past six years. Her articles feature a mix of child development and Native American philosophy and are available for browsing on her web site: www.parenting-child-development.com. Laura also writes about child discipline, learning disabilities, family values and the joys and challenges of raising children.

Order Form

Fax Orders: 775-856-4277 (Fax completed form.)
Email Orders: info@parenting-child-development.com
Web Orders: www.parenting-child-development.com

Please send me:
_____*Keepers of the Children* by Laura Ramirez @ $18.95
_____*Keepers of the Children E-Workbook* by Laura Ramirez @ $14.95
_____Sign me up to receive *The Circle* Newsletter @ $29.95

Name:_____

Address:_____

City:_____State:_____ Zip:_____

Telephone:_____Email:_____
Please add 7.75% sales tax for orders shipped to destinations in
Nevada.

Shipping by air:
United States: $4.95 for first book and $2.00 for each additional.
International: $10.95 for first book; $6.00 for each additional. (This is
an estimate. Customer will be charged actual cost.)

Please check form of payment:

_____ Check _____ Credit Card #_____
Expiration:_____ 4 digit code on back_____
_____ Mastercard _____ Visa _____ American Express

Name on card:_____

Signature: _____

CPSIA information can be obtained at www.ICGtesting.com
Printed in the USA
BVOW012145291111

277191BV00003B/102/A